Howard Conkling

Mexico and the Mexicans

Notes of travel in the winter and spring of 1883

Howard Conkling

Mexico and the Mexicans
Notes of travel in the winter and spring of 1883

ISBN/EAN: 9783337257651

Printed in Europe, USA, Canada, Australia, Japan

Cover: Foto ©Andreas Hilbeck / pixelio.de

More available books at **www.hansebooks.com**

THE CATHEDRAL, MEXICO.

Mexico and the Mexicans

OR,

NOTES OF TRAVEL IN THE WINTER
AND SPRING OF 1883.

BY

HOWARD CONKLING.

WITH ILLUSTRATIONS.

NEW YORK:
TAINTOR BROTHERS, MERRILL & CO.
1883.

PREFACE.

Among the most vivid and cherished memories of my childhood are the descriptions which my grandfather, after his return from his mission as Minister to Mexico, was accustomed to give of that land of mystery and romance. What especially dazzled my imagination was the picture he drew of that world-renowned landmark of the navigator, the snow-capped peak of Orizaba, which, as the war-steamer that bore him to his destination neared the Mexican coast, stood out like a gigantic spectre against the clear blue sky. So, too, with the matchless view, from the *plateau* near Ario, of the marvellous volcano of Jorullo, which, almost within the memory of living men, sprang up, as if at the command of an enchanter, to the height of more than four thousand feet, amid the palm, the banana, the orange, and the lemon groves of the Pacific slope.

Not less fascinating was his description of the gorgeous hues of the flowers, the splendid coloring of the butterflies, and the brilliant plumage of the birds; all of which seemed like pictures of fairy-land.

Nor have I forgotten the testimony which he bore to the high courtesy with which he was everywhere received and treated, in social, as well as in official circles.

Now that the bonds of friendship and alliance between our own country and our sister Republic are about to be drawn so much closer; now that a new, auspicious, and even brilliant era is about to dawn upon the Land of the Aztecs, I made up my mind, in the month of January last, to see Mexico with my own eyes.

The succeeding pages contain the record of my observations and experiences during my recent tour through that country. I have endeavored to portray the condition of the Mexican people, under their social, industrial and religious aspects, and to present a brief sketch of their commercial, agricultural, mining and other industrial interests.

I gladly avail myself of this opportunity to record my grateful sense of obligation to Señor Don Matias Romero, the Mexican Minister at Washington, for the valuable aid, in the prosecution of my plans, with which he has so kindly favored me. With the politeness which so well befits his eminent station, he not only furnished me with letters of introduction to General Manuel Gonzalez, the President of the United Mexican States, and to various other gentlemen of official and social distinction, but he has likewise supplied me with official documents, of great importance and value, which were not otherwise accessible. Indeed, but for my reliance upon his long-standing friendship for my father and uncle, I should have hesitated to undertake the preparation of these pages.

What the future has in store for the human family, Providence has wisely hidden from our view. Still, it may be said that many indications point to the early federation of all the peoples that now inhabit the North American Continent. Hence I look forward to the meeting of the gentleman from the Isthmus of Panama with the gentleman from the frozen zone, on the floor of the Capitol at Washington, to exchange congratulations that the government of North America is, and will forever remain, one and indivisible.

CONTENTS.

	PAGE
DEDICATION	iii
PREFACE	v
I. FROM NEW YORK TO ESPERANZA	1
II. AGRICULTURE	16
III. PUEBLA AND CHOLULA	28
IV. MEXICAN HISTORY	41
V. THE CITY OF MEXICO	66
VI. THE SERPENT-WORSHIP	90
VII. VISITS TO PROMINENT PERSONS	102
VIII. A TRIP WESTWARD	112
IX. THE VOLCANO OF JORULLO	135
X. CUERNAVACA	153
XI. COMMERCE	159
XII. SAN JUAN TEOTIHUACAN	170
XIII. ASCENT OF THE GREAT VOLCANO	178
XIV. QUERETARO.—MR. SEWARD'S VISIT	192
XV. THE NORTHERN CITIES	206
XVI. MINING	223

Contents.

		PAGE
XVII.	TO AND FROM SAN LUIS POTOSI	235
XVIII.	THROUGH THE SIERRA MADRE	248
XIX.	THE RAILROADS	256
XX.	THE RAILROADS—*Continued*	269
XXI.	MONTEREY	283
XXII.	THE FUTURE OF MEXICO	288

LIST OF ILLUSTRATIONS.

	PAGE
THE CATHEDRAL, MEXICO............... *Frontispiece.*	
SACRED SERPENT.....................................	91
QUETZALCOATL.......................................	91
THE GODDESS TEOYAOMIQUI........................	92
VOLCANO OF JORULLO...............................	135
POPOCATEPETL.......................................	180
IZTACCIHUATL	180

MEXICO AND THE MEXICANS.

CHAPTER I.

FROM NEW YORK TO ESPERANZA.

IN the month of January last I left New York, with its wintry climate, and after a pleasant and speedy journey by rail, I found myself in the balmy atmosphere of Florida. Then I took my way to the old Creole city of New Orleans, and embarked for Vera Cruz, the principal port of Mexico. While on the voyage the ship encountered one of those hurricanes which occur periodically on the Gulf of Mexico, and which are known by the name of "Northers"; but it was attended with no more serious consequences than the sea-sickness of most of the passengers. On the morning of the sixth day after leaving port the steamer dropped anchor under the walls of the fortress of San Juan de Ulloa (now dismantled, and used as a state prison,), which is situated on a small island off Vera Cruz, and which affords a partial shelter to vessels in stormy weather. When a severe " Norther " is in progress all vessels are obliged to put to sea and wait for the troubled waters to subside. The anchorage is so shallow that all communication with the shore must be had by small boats. The coral reefs which everywhere abound make the navigation very dangerous, and the numerous wrecks serve to admonish shipmasters to proceed with the utmost caution when approaching the coast.

No sooner had the steamer dropped anchor than it was surrounded by a fleet of small boats, rowed by men of every conceivable shade of complexion (white alone excepted), who swarmed up the sides of the good ship " City of Mexico," and offered their services to land passengers and baggage. Having engaged one of these men, I was presently landed at the Custom House, where my trunk and valise were promptly examined by a polite and obliging officer. Thereupon my boatman, placing them on a curious two-wheeled vehicle drawn by three mules abreast, led the way to the Hôtel de Diligencias.

The port of Vera Cruz, which has a population of about twelve thousand souls, has for centuries been the sole Mexican portal, on the Gulf side, for the commerce of the world. Its streets are narrow, and are laid out at right angles; the houses are built of coral rock covered with stucco. They are two stories in height, the first story being used for business purposes and the second as the family residence of the occupant. The centre of the lot is arranged as a court-yard, sometimes very tastefully laid out and planted with tropical trees, plants, and flowers. There is one street railway. The cars are drawn by two undersized mules, and the driver announces his approach by blowing a horn.

Everything centres around the Plaza de la Constitucion, a park about two hundred feet square. It is the one redeeming feature of the city, and its cocoanut palms, its laurel-trees, and its fountains form a pleasant contrast to the white stucco of the Hôtel de Diligencias, the parochial church, and the other buildings surrounding it. At night it is lighted by electric lights. Owing to the absence of all sewerage, and the drainage consisting solely of a kennel in the centre of the streets, the atmosphere is invariably loaded with poisonous exhalations. As might be expected in that torrid climate, the yellow fever prevails there at all seasons of the year in a malignant form. Of course the first and most engrossing care of the stranger is to make his escape, at the earliest possible moment, from its pestilential courts.

At six o'clock on the morning succeeding my arrival, I took passage on the Mexican Railway, which extends from the city of Vera Cruz to the Mexican capital, a distance of two hundred and sixty-four miles, thus overcoming an elevation of seven thousand three hundred and fifty feet, and even ascending, in one part of the route, to an elevation of eight thousand three hundred and thirty-three feet. As the train was about to leave the station, a squad of twenty-five soldiers under the command of an officer, who took their places in the forward car, suggested the possible danger of robbers along the route.

Running rapidly across the plain of the *Tierras Calientes*, or Hot Lands, the train ascended in rapid succession a number of very steep grades, and passing through a short tunnel, suddenly emerged upon a landscape of enchanting beauty. It was an undulating plateau surrounded by mountains; while the lofty peak of Orizaba, which formed the background, seemed to meet the sky.

I soon passed the town of Cordova, which is noted for its numerous and extensive coffee-plantations. Epicures have pronounced the coffee here produced to surpass, in the delicacy of its flavor, any other in the world, the far-famed berry of Mocha not excepted.

And now the train approaches the great chasm of Metlac. Here the railroad presents a wonderful exhibition of engineering skill. Running upon a very steep grade along the side of a mountain, the passenger who looks down sees no object intervening between the car and the bottom of the gulf, some five hundred or six hundred feet below. Farther on, where the ravine is not so deep, it is spanned by an iron bridge. After crossing, the train runs back in the opposite direction over a similar steep grade, having made a complete horse-shoe curve to accomplish the passage of the ravine. In point of grandeur and engineering skill this work far surpasses the famous horse-shoe curve of the Pennsylvania Railroad, which was constructed for a similar purpose.

An hour's ride from Metlac brought me to Orizaba. I had come ninety miles from Vera Cruz, ascending four thousand and twenty-seven feet, and found myself in the midst of a region so surpassingly beautiful as almost to form a terrestrial paradise. Marshal Bazaine made his head-quarters here during the French occupation of Mexico, and it thus became the most important centre of that freebooter's military operations.

Orizaba has a population of seventeen thousand. There is a street railway, with branches extending in various directions, and it is used for the transportation of freight as well as passengers. The streets are wide, and are laid out at right angles. The houses are covered with stucco, and are roofed with tiles of a dull red color. Their height seldom exceeds a single story, the windows, which extend almost to the ground, being secured with iron gratings. There is a very good hotel here, kept by a young German widow. Her late and lamented husband had been a lieutenant in Maximilian's army. She has been regarded by connoisseurs as the prettiest woman in Mexico.

On the northern side of the town, a hill which rises about fifteen hundred feet above the plain commands an admirable view of the place and its environs. The prospect from its summit is exceedingly grand. Imagine a plain of unsurpassed fertility, extending about ten miles in every direction, covered with rich fields of sugarcane, tobacco, and Indian corn, and situated within an amphitheatre of high mountains, above which rises majestically the lofty peak of Orizaba.

The town is situated in the centre of the plain, and the monotonous white buildings with red roofs are relieved not only by the verdure of a most luxuriant semi-tropical vegetation in the plazas and court-yards which abound in every part of the town, but also by the spires and domes of the churches. There are ten of these edifices; a rather large number, it would seem to us, for a population of seventeen thousand souls. I ought to add, however, that since President Juarez and his successors have abridged the power and privileges of the Church, several of these edifices have been used for secular purposes, while others have been altogether abandoned, and are rapidly falling into decay.

The climate of Orizaba in winter is uniform and delightful. It was still February, yet the heat of the sun, at mid-day, was somewhat oppressive. The mornings and evenings, however, were comparatively cool. During the warmer portions of the day the clothing of the inhabitants consists of only a single thickness of cotton cloth; but as the sun declines, they cover themselves with a blanket, sometimes thrown over the shoulders, and sometimes with the head inserted through a slit provided for that purpose.

These blankets, costing much less than an overcoat, are useful as a covering by night as well as by day. The principal part of the population of Mexico, it may be remarked, is descended from the aborigines, and has little or no admixture of European blood. To-day we have the same race which the Spanish conqueror Cortez found here more than three centuries ago, with only such changes as foreign rulers have imposed upon them. There is nothing surprising, therefore, in the circumstance that they dress so much like the aboriginal population of the United States.

The citizens of Orizaba never tire of boasting about their famous cataract. They exhort travellers never to think of going away till they have visited this grand natural curiosity. It must be acknowledged, however, that the tourist who has not become familiar with the physical geography óf Mexico is hardly qualified to sympathize with their admiration. To those who have seen the Eureka Falls, Buttermilk Falls, High Falls, and other such spectacles which are exhibited at almost every rural watering-place in this country, the high-sounding praises of the little cascade near the suburb of Jalapilla will seem to be greatly exaggerated. But after they have travelled through Mexico and noticed the extreme scarcity of water, and especially of running streams, more particularly on the tablelands, they will be able to appreciate the pride and enthusiasm of the people of Orizaba.

When I visited the cascade I entered a lumbering vehicle of tremendous avoirdupois and great antiquity, drawn by mules. It was so heavy that the mules were unable to pull it up the first hill, and as it began that unpleasant motion of running backward down hill, everybody jumped out and lent a helping hand. The road lies through magnificent fields of sugar-cane and passes a *hacienda* building where the operation of crushing the cane and manufacturing molasses may be seen. The superintendent received me with great courtesy, and accompanied me through the establishment.

While at Orizaba the opportunity was afforded me to witness the favorite national amusement—a bull-fight. It was on Sunday, which is a gala day in Mexico, and the proceeds of the entertainment were devoted to charity. The ring was built inside the walls of a deserted church edifice. Seats in the shade commanded a higher price than those in the sun. Of the women who honored the entertainment with their presence, very few could lay claim to an elevated social position; and, strange to say, the costume of these was not of a kind to attract any attention. Not so with the men. Every variety of attire that could gratify personal vanity seemed to be here represented. *Sombreros* trimmed with silver cord, which sometimes almost covered up the entire hat, and tight-fitting black trousers, with the outside seams decorated with silver chains laid crosswise, and terminating in little balls or buttons, were favorite articles of adornment. Some of the spectators came on horses with very elaborately ornamented saddles. A gentleman showed me a saddle, inlaid with gold, which he valued at a thousand dollars.

A very good band was in attendance, and presently the *toreadores*, or bull-fighters, entered the arena. These were dressed in handsome costumes of fantastical colors. A door being thrown open, the bull rushed in and charged the various actors, who maddened him by flaunting red flags before his eyes, and who, with great agility, would avoid his horns by springing lightly to one side. When too closely pressed they would take refuge behind a small but substantial board fence, provided at several places, at a distance of about one foot and a half from the sides of the ring, thus affording them a refuge which is too small for the bull to enter. The bull next gave his attention to the *picador*, who is a horseman armed with a somewhat blunt spear. In this instance his horse was protected from the horns of the bull by a heavy piece of sole leather hung over the chest. As the bull was about to strike the horse the *picador* fastened his spear in the bull's shoulder and forced him away. At every repeated onslaught the *picador* with unerring dexterity put his spear into the wound so made, and held the infuriated animal at bay. Perhaps his ability to check the bull's furious charges was due rather to the pain caused by the stroke than to the strength of his arm.

Then men on foot, called *banderilleros*, came forward with their *banderillas*, which are barbed weapons to which are fastened ribbons or bright-colored pieces of paper, and which must be stuck into the animal's neck. This must be done by coming up directly in front, and not by any stealthy approach from behind. Of course the feat is attended with a considerable amount of personal risk. One of the *banderilleros* was knocked down and trampled upon, but his companions immediately advanced and, with their flags, diverted the bull's attention, which gave him time to rise and make good his escape.

When the spectators had been sufficiently amused by all this brutality, the bull was dispatched by the long straight sword of the *matador*, who with one thrust pierced the animal's heart. He was then dragged away, the band meanwhile making as much noise as possible. This routine is repeated half a dozen times. When a fresh bull does not show a warlike disposition he is lassoed and taken away.

My next departure was taken for Esperanza. The railway runs along the side of the mountain, which towers aloft to the height of two thousand feet, and enters a narrow cañon of great depth, made the more conspicuous by numerous advertisements of Saint Jacob's Oil in the Spanish language. After several windings the train gained the summit, which commands one of the most magnificent prospects of the kind in the world.

A stop is had at Boca del Monte, an altitude of seven thousand nine hundred and twenty-four feet, which marks the dividing line between the States of Vera Cruz and Puebla.

Esperanza is a railway station, with a good hotel, kept by a Frenchman, and is fifteen miles distant from the volcano of Orizaba. Here I had the good fortune to make the acquaintance of Señor Don Camillo Averami, the manager of an extensive *hacienda*, or plantation. With the courtesy characteristic of his countrymen he conducted me over the estate. He had many square miles of land under cultivation, and had, besides, vast herds of cattle, flocks of sheep, and droves of mules. He had a large counting-house, with several clerks; also shops, stores, and all necessary appurtenances, giving employment and subsistence to two hundred families. The laborers occupied cabins on the estate, and a church and school were provided for them and their children. My friend, the *haciendado*, rode a splendid white horse, elegantly caparisoned, and was attired in the showy costume of the country. Everywhere the people paid court to him as to a prince, and several of them, at his command, joined us. We spent the first night on the floor of a laborer's cabin, the second in a cave on the mountain-side—the entire trip occupying nearly three days.

CHAPTER II.

AGRICULTURE.

The physical geography of Mexico is perhaps more remarkable than that of any other portion of the earth's surface of equal extent. Stretching through seventeen degrees of latitude and thirty degrees of longitude, comprising a superficial area of eight hundred and thirty thousand square miles, or nearly eighteen times as great as that of the State of New York, a large portion of which is unsurpassed in fertility, her soil yields the products of every zone and climate between the Equator and the North Pole. But this is not all: owing to a peculiar combination of heat and moisture, extensive districts produce each year two crops of Indian corn, of wheat, and of the other cereals which are common to the Temperate Zone. Thus it would seem that Mexico is singularly favored of heaven with all the natural conditions required to make her the home of a numerous and prosperous people.

The configuration of this vast region and its climatic conditions have suggested its division into three several parts—the *Tierras Calientes*, the *Tierras Templadas*, and the *Tierras Frias*. The *Tierras Calientes*, or Hot Lands, include the low grounds, or those having an elevation of less than two thousand five hundred feet above the sea-level, on the east and west coasts. The *Tierras Calientes* of the west are not so extensive as those of the east, the western arm of the Cordilleras approaching nearer to the sea. This great mountain chain traverses the whole length of Mexico. On the northern border of Guatemala it bifurcates—the western arm following the coast of the Pacific, and the eastern arm that of the Gulf of Mexico, subsiding into the plains of Texas. The annual mean temperature of this region is estimated at seventy-seven degrees Fahrenheit, which especially adapts it to the growth and cultivation of all the agricultural products requiring a high temperature, such as sugar-cane, vanilla, indigo, tobacco, cotton, and bananas.

The *Tierras Templadas*, or Temperate Lands, which are of comparatively limited extent, occupy the slopes of the mountain ranges which have been referred to, and the regions adjacent thereto. They extend from about two thousand five hundred feet to five thousand feet in elevation, and the mean temperature does not vary essentially from sixty-eight degrees. The extremes of heat and cold are alike unknown to the inhabitants of these delightful regions. All the trees, fruits, flowers, and cereals of the United States flourish in this climate.

The *Tierras Frias*, or Cold Lands, include the vast plateau, elevated five thousand feet and upward above the sea. In the City of Mexico, at an elevation of seven thousand three hundred and fifty feet, the thermometer sometimes falls below the freezing point, and consequently snow-storms occasionally occur. In the coldest season of the year the mean temperature of the day varies from fifty-five to seventy degrees, while in summer the thermometer seldom rises in the shade above seventy-five degrees. The annual mean temperature may be taken at sixty-two degrees; but wherever the table-land rises to more than eight thousand feet it has, even in that portion which lies within the tropics, a somewhat rigorous climate. Under the parallel of the City of Mexico the limit of perpetual snow varies from fourteen thousand five hundred feet to fifteen thousand feet.

In the tropical and central regions, and as far north as the latitude of twenty-eight degrees, there are only two seasons—that of rain, lasting from June to the middle of September; and the dry season, continuing from October to the end of May. In some portions of the table-land, however, showers, and even protracted rains, sometimes occur during the dry season. In the month of February, during my sojourn in the City of Mexico, heavy showers frequently occurred during three successive days; and at Maravatio, on my journey to visit the great volcano of Jorullo, a copious rain fell during an entire day and night. In travelling by rail from Vera Cruz to the capital, every variety of climate is experienced within the space of a few hours; and the natural productions peculiar to each zone are successively passed in review, from the sugar-cane, indigo plant, and bananas of the tropics, to the pines, firs, and lichens of the far north.

These peculiar conditions of topography and climate offer unrivalled advantages for the cultivation of Indian corn, the cereals, coffee, cocoa, sugar, cotton, and tobacco; and, except on the northern part of the central plateau, there are splendid timber lands, especially on the mountain slopes. The flora is exceedingly rich and extensive, more than ten thousand families of plants having been recognized. The flowers are surpassingly beautiful and graceful in their structure, exquisite in color, and of wonderful fragrance.

The cultivation of Indian corn is by far the most important branch of agricultural industry. The official statistics show that in the fiscal year of 1879 the total value of the agricultural products of the country, comprising twenty-six several articles, was $177,451,986, of which the value of the corn crop was $112,164,424, or more than three-fifths of the entire amount. The production of brown beans in the same year equalled in value $8,406,211. Indian corn and brown beans constitute almost the sole articles of food of an overwhelming majority of the entire population. Next in importance to the cultivation of Indian corn is that of wheat, and the amount of its production is given at $17,436,345.

Tobacco is extensively grown in the States of Chiapas, Tabasco, and Vera Cruz. That produced in the State of Tabasco is considered the best, its quality being unsurpassed by that of the choicest Cuban tobacco. At no distant day the growth and exportation of this article will prove to be a source of immense revenue. The railroad which is about to be constructed, under the immediate auspices of General U. S. Grant, will run through these tobacco growing districts, thus providing them with the facilities of transportation which at present they so greatly need.

It is hardly to be expected that Mexican cotton will ever become an important article of export. It is inferior in staple to that grown in the United States; but the quality and quantity produced will doubtless suffice for the greater part of the home consumption.

The coffee-tree requires a climate which is exempt from frost on the one hand and from excessive heat on the other. It grows best on the hills, and where it is partially shaded from the sun's rays. The leaves of the banana-tree often answer that purpose. It is safe to say that nowhere else in the world can a region be found which can compete with the less elevated regions of the *Tierras Templadas* in the growth of this important article, which, like sugar, is consumed about equally by the prince and the peasant, and the demand for which is consequently almost unlimited.

It is to be borne in mind that the preceding remarks apply to the *Tierras Calientes* and to the *Tierras Templadas,* and not to the *Tierras Frias.* The latter comprise not less than three-fifths of the entire area of the country. The greater portion of this vast region is susceptible of culture only under unfavorable and expensive conditions. The historian Prescott describes it with his accustomed accuracy and elegance of diction. "Across this mountain rampart," he says, "a chain of volcanic hills stretches, in a westerly direction, of still more stupendous dimensions, forming, indeed, some of the highest land on the globe. Their peaks, entering the limits of perpetual snow, diffuse a grateful coolness over the elevated plateaus below; for these last, though termed 'cold,' enjoy a climate the mean temperature of which is not lower than that of the central parts of Italy. The air is exceedingly dry; the soil, though naturally good, is rarely clothed with the luxuriant vegetation of the lower regions. It frequently, indeed, has a parched and barren aspect, owing partly to the greater evaporation which takes place on these lofty plains, through the diminished pressure of the atmosphere; and partly, no doubt, to the want of trees to shelter the soil from the fierce influence of the summer sun. In the time of the Aztecs the table-land was thickly covered with larch, oak, cypress, and other forest trees, the extraordinary dimensions of some of which, remaining to the present day, show that the curse of barrenness, in later times, is chargeable more on man than on nature. Indeed, the early Spaniards made an indiscriminate war on the forest, as did our Puritan ancestors, though with much less reason. After once conquering the country they had no lurking ambush to fear from the submissive, semi-civilized Indian, and were not, like our forefathers, obliged to keep watch and ward for a century. The spoliation of the ground, however, is said to have been pleasant to their imaginations, as it reminded them of the plains of their own Castile—the table-land of Europe, where the nakedness of the landscape forms the burden of every traveller's lament, who visits that country."

Whether in the future the grand plateau is to be brought under cultivation will depend chiefly upon the restoration of at least a portion of the forests with which it was once clothed. The annual rain-fall in the City of Mexico is estimated by Humboldt to be fifty-nine inches, while in San Francisco it is only twenty, and in the City of New York is but forty-five, inches. Yet, denuded as the immense plain has been of its timber, the copious rains, which chiefly fall during four months of the year, are carried off by the mountain torrents, leaving the country parched, except where it is made fruitful by irrigation. Be this as it may, it is satisfactory to know that the *Tierras Frias* are admirably adapted to the raising of horses, horned cattle, and sheep.

The agricultural interests of Mexico, irrespective of the great plain, are susceptible of the greatest development, a comparatively small proportion of the arable lands of the country being under cultivation, and the methods of labor employed being of the most primitive kinds. At present, however, the farmer has no motive materially to increase the yield of his lands, as he is unable to export his produce with advantage, owing to the expensive and inadequate facilities of transportation which are at his command. Except in the case of the few railways which have been, up to this time, constructed, nearly all merchandise must be transported on the backs of men, mules, or donkeys. Thus the exportation of agricultural produce, on account of the attendant expense and labor, is rendered almost impracticable. Hence the annual production of many articles exceeds by only a very small amount the limit of the quantity required to supply the home markets. In the fiscal year of 1879 there was produced $8,761,317 worth of sugar, and tobacco of the value of $2,006,153. These two articles aggregate $10,767,470, and yet the value of their annual exportation does not usually exceed $600,000. In the year 1882 the value was $617,000.

The ingenuity of the thinking men of Mexico has for a long time been exercised in trying to devise some means whereby domestic and foreign trade may be stimulated, and the agricultural resources of the country may be developed. The President of the Republic thinks that the most urgent need of the country is the construction of cheap roads, in conjunction with the railway system, by which the national products may be transported on reasonable terms. This, he thinks, would assure the production and profitable exportation of all the articles which can be raised on the rich soil of the country. That traffic once placed upon a firm financial basis, he believes that an era of unprecedented national prosperity would ensue.

CHAPTER III.

PUEBLA AND CHOLULA.

From Esperanza to the City of Mexico the railroad runs through a sandy plain, a small portion of which is utterly barren. On several occasions I observed columns of sand drawn up, by a whirlwind, to a height of several hundred feet, and then dispersed in suffocating clouds. At such times horsemen cover their mouths and noses with scarfs, or draw up their blankets, to protect their lungs. I may here remark that it appears to be a national custom to cover the lower part of the face in the cooler portions of the day.

At Apizaco I took the branch railroad for Puebla. In size and population this is the third city in the Republic, containing about seventy-five thousand inhabitants. It is situated on a plain between the volcano of Malinche, which is ten miles distant on one side, and the volcanoes of Popocatepetl and Iztaccihuatl, twenty-five miles distant in the opposite direction. It was founded by the Spaniards in 1531, and is now an important commercial and manufacturing emporium. Its churches are justly regarded as superior to those of most of the other cities of the Republic. I attended high mass at the elegant church of La Compania. The music was grand and solemn. Indeed, the music in Mexican churches is always of a high order. The cathedral is on one side of the grand plaza, in the centre of the city. Its architecture is superior to that of many of the celebrated cathedrals in the capitals of Europe. The structure is extensive, with two lofty towers in front, a large dome at the centre, and another at the rear. The interior is beautifully frescoed, and profusely supplied with every variety of ecclesiastical ornamentation. External niches in the walls are filled with the statues of the saints and martyrs of Jesus.

On the other three sides of the plaza are buildings with arcades, as in the Rue de Rivoli in Paris. These arcades are occupied by the stands of venders of fruit and small wares, and also by the tables of professional letter-writers, who offer their services to their less educated countrymen.

The principal hotel is very comfortable, and the manager was very polite and obliging. It is a two-story building with a *porte cochère*, and a square court-yard in the centre, embellished with plants and trees. The front rooms on the first floor are occupied as shops, and the rear part of the building is used as a stable. On the second floor a wide gallery extends around the court-yard, and it answers the double purpose of office and dining halls. The sleeping apartments open off the gallery, and, the hotel being situated on a corner, many of them front on the street, where the windows are provided with small balconies.

The Paseo de San Francisco, at the northern end of the city, is a small park, a half mile long and about two hundred feet wide. It affords both a delightful promenade and short carriage drive. The Church of San Francisco, near the entrance, is very noticeable for the style of its architecture. The façade is of carved stone, and the other portions of the edifice are built of brick, adorned in places with colored and pictured tiles of every variety.

The College of the State of Puebla offers educational facilities for one thousand students. The system of instruction is very thorough, and the student can enter upon almost any course of study which he desires.

Taking the horse-car, I visited the town of Cholula, which is between seven and eight miles distant from Puebla, and was formerly the capital of the province, as well as the religious metropolis of Mexico. Its history illustrates in a striking manner the mutability of human affairs. When Cortez first entered it he estimated the number of houses within the walls at twenty thousand, and as many more in the environs, making the population at least one hundred and fifty thousand. Now the number of inhabitants does not exceed ten thousand. Once conspicuous for its trade, manufactures, wealth and splendor, now desolation and silence reign supreme on every side. A church built by Cortez contains a series of historical paintings illustrative of the epoch of the Conquest, and is well worth the attention of the tourist. The immense pyramid which stands here is supposed to be the oldest in Mexico, and possesses the greatest interest for the scholastic theologian, as well as for the archæologist. It is built of sun-dried bricks alternated with layers of clay, and its dimensions far exceed those of every other structure ever reared by human hands. Indeed, the only memorials of the past which in size bear any comparison to it are the colossal mounds the remains of which are still extant on the banks of the Euphrates. According to Humboldt, its base-line originally measured one thousand four hundred and twenty-three feet, or more than double the length of the Great Pyramid of Cheops, thus covering an area of upwards of forty-four acres. Its height is still one hundred and seventy-seven feet, although one of its four terraces has succumbed to the ravages of time. The superficial area of the platform, on its summit, exceeds an acre in extent. It remains to be said, and I record the fact not without some degree of sorrow and indignation, that the hand of the utilitarian has not spared this most wonderful monument. In order to avoid a slight detour, a cut for the track of the horse railroad has been made through one portion of it, while a considerable part of the base has been levelled and placed under cultivation. Nevertheless, it still stands pre-eminent among the monuments of an unknown antiquity.

The Aztec conquerors of Mexico found it standing there with its shrine upon its summit; but no trustworthy record or tradition concerning the date of its erection has come down to our time. I have often wondered what may have been said of it in the imperial archives of ancient Tenochtitlan, and in the thousands of books which were ruthlessly destroyed by the Spanish propagandists of the religion of the Prince of Peace. It has been very plausibly ascribed to the Toltecs, or to the earlier Olmecs, and by some its construction is supposed to have been coeval with the commencement of the Christian era. One Aztec tradition, preserved by the learned Jesuit father Torquemada, has assigned to it an origin analogous to that of the Tower of Babel in the land of Shinar. It relates that one of the seven demi-gods, who escaped from a great deluge by climbing to the top of Mount Tlaloc, began the building of this pyramid to commemorate that event. He intended that its summit should reach the clouds, but the gods were angry at his presumption, and dispersed the workmen with lightning.

Mr. Baldwin, in his interesting work on Ancient America, expresses the opinion that this pyramid was built by the Toltecs, and that it is of the same general character as the mounds found in the more northern portions of this continent, and as the temples of Central America. He chiefly relies upon the testimony of M. Brasseur de Bourbourg, and his translation of the *Popul-Vuh*, an old record of the preceding inhabitants. The Toltecs, we are informed, were the same race that once occupied the valleys of the Ohio and Mississippi, working the copper mines of Lake Superior, and erecting the various mounds and earthworks that still exist throughout all that region. They were obliged to leave that country, probably on account of the hostility of other and more warlike tribes. A sentence in one of the hieroglyphical records of Central America seems to give an air of plausibility to this theory. It states that the Toltecs emigrated from Ancient Tlapallan, a very distant country at the northeast, more than two thousand years ago. Mr. Baldwin suggests that this race were the builders of the Great Pyramid of Cholula, and that the inhabitants of the surrounding region, at the coming of the Spaniards, belonged to that race. After their subjugation by the Aztecs, Cholula became a sanctuary and sacred resort for pilgrims and worshippers from all parts of Mexico. It surpassed all other cities in distinction and sanctity. As, in ancient Assyria, the conquered Akkads became the scribes and priests of the country, so the Cholulans seem to have become the sacred caste of Mexico.

The Teocalli,* or the Great Pyramid, was not the only shrine in the Holy City. Other races there

---

* Literally—The House of God ; in other words, the pyramid on which the human sacrifices were offered.

founded numerous temples; and Cortez relates that he counted four hundred turrets, some temples having two and others only one, to indicate them. Thus it would seem that Cholula was the Aztec Hierapolis. Religious processions, sacrifices and festivals were of almost continual occurrence. No other city had so great a concourse of priests, and so incessant a round of ceremonies. It was thronged by pilgrims from all parts of Anahuac; and while the poor painfully begged their way thither, and subsisted while there upon charitable contributions, the city was enriched and adorned by the benefactions of the more opulent worshippers. Thus the sacred city of the Cholulans was to this continent what Rome, Delphi, and Mecca were to the old.

Quetzalcoatl was the divinity whose worship was celebrated in the shrine of the Great Pyramid. Tradition accords to him the distinction of being the civilizer of the Aztec race. He was the god of the sky, and bore a cross to denote his dominion over the four winds. His worship did not originate with the Aztecs, for they had derived it from the more ancient and refined

Mayas and Central Americans. Kukulkan and Gukumutz, their designations of this deity, have the same meaning. He was the central figure of the Toltec mythology. Like Apollo in the Grecian, and Krishna in Brahmanical mythology, he is always represented as having dwelt with mankind. The legends give him both a human and a divine parentage. He had been born of a virgin in ancient Tula or Tlapallan, and became the supreme pontiff of that region. Coming from the East, he brought science and the arts with him for the enlightenment of the races of Mexico and Central America. Glowing descriptions are given of his reign and the numerous blessings which characterized it. He established agriculture, he taught the textile arts, and instituted religious worship. This was the golden age of Anahuac, and the most romantic fables of its prosperity are recorded. Finally, however, this period came to an end. He proclaimed that he had been summoned home to Tlapallan. A legend declares that the divinity Tezcatlipoca, or Yoallichecatl, the spirit of night, had given him a drink, under the pretence that it would render him immortal; but it had only awakened in his breast an uncontrollable longing for home. He accordingly entered his boat of serpent-skins, and sailed away—that is, he departed on a cloud with the lightning, promising, however, to return from the East and again reign over Anahuac.

Thus the second advent of Quetzalcoatl was regarded by the Mexicans with sentiments and expectations akin to those of the Hebrews relative to their promised Messiah. The latter expected a temporal prince who should vanquish every enemy, who should exalt the Israelitish nation to a degree of power and splendor surpassing the glorious epoch of David and Solomon, and who should make the holy city on Mount Zion the seat of empire to which the wealth of the nations would flow, and kings would come to render homage. With like confidence and fervor the ancient inhabitants of Mexico looked forward to the return of their divine monarch Quetzalcoatl, with his family and court, to resume and perpetuate his temporal and spiritual dominion at Cholula. The Spaniards were greatly aided in their operations by the belief, which was nearly universal among the peoples of Anahuac, that the day and the hour of the second advent of their Messiah was at hand. Earthquakes, inundations, conflagrations, and comets had followed each other in rapid succession. Strange lights had been seen in the heavens, and mysterious voices had been heard in the air. Observing these signs, all the oracles, seers, soothsayers and astrologers concurred in prognosticating that a terrible calamity was about to overtake the Aztec dynasty.

When the Spaniards landed on the shores of his empire, a report in picture-writing was at once transmitted to Montezuma. He recognized in its symbols the fulfilment of the predicted return of Quetzalcoatl, and was overwhelmed wi h consternation. This report represented that men of fair complexions and flowing beards had arrived from the East in vast "water-houses," and that they rode upon mysterious four-footed beasts, and held in their hands the thunder and the lightning. These facts, coinciding as they did with their traditions, seemed to indicate to the Aztecs the divine origin of the visitors; and the belief soon became general that the great chief who sent greetings to Montezuma was none other than the divine Quetzalcoatl returned with his retinue to resume possession of his empire. In looking upon the faces of the down-trodden and submissive peons, I have sometimes doubted whether their minds and hearts had ever become fully emancipated from this impression. Be this as it may, it is easy to understand how this superstition facilitated the march of the Spaniards to victory and dominion.

It was now time to bid farewell to this supposed earthly abode of the benign god of the air and return to the dwelling-place of common men. I did not wait for the coming of the vehicle which, on its rounds, had brought me hither. The day was fine and the road good. I accordingly set out on foot, and, walking vigorously, arrived at my hotel while it was yet early.

The next day, taking the train for Apizaco, the point of junction with the main line of the Mexican Railway, I proceeded directly to the capital of Mexico.

CHAPTER IV.

MEXICAN HISTORY.

The early history of Mexico is hidden in the twilight of fable. That illustrious explorer, scientist, and scholar, Alexander von Humboldt, has traced it back to the seventh century of the Christian era. He states that the Toltecs appeared in the year 648; the Chichemecs in 1170; the Nahuas in 1178; the Acolhuas and Aztecs in 1196. Their respective languages show that all of them belonged to the same family with the other aboriginal races of North America. The Toltecs came first and developed a high civilization. They introduced the culture of cotton and Indian corn. They constructed highways and bridges, and they built cities. They erected the pyramids which are yet the wonder and admiration of the world. They employed hieroglyphical writing, reduced and wrought the metals, skilfully carved the hardest stones, and were proficient in astronomical learning. Their solar calendar was more perfect than that of the Greeks and Romans. They are said to have finally retired from the country to Central America, and the Chichemecs, a wild race, occupied the territory which they had abandoned. The Nahuas soon followed them, and after them, at the end of the twelfth century, the Aztec conquerors took possession of the Valley of Anahuac. For more than a century they appear not to have had any fixed abode. For a time they were enslaved by the Colhuas, but they finally succeeded in regaining their freedom.

The earliest legend represents them as now tired of a roving life, and desirous of founding a city. Their oracle commanded them to do this where they should see an eagle standing on a cactus which grew upon a rock. This omen was witnessed on the Lake Tezcuco, and accordingly, in the year 1325, they there founded the city, and named it Tenochtitlan, which signifies a cactus and a stone. The founders of the existing Republic further perpetuated the tradition by adopting the device of the eagle and cactus, which forms the national coat-of-arms of Mexico.

After the conquest by the Spaniards, the more civilized people of the southern region preferred to endure the foreign yoke to encountering the privation and perils of emigration; while the northern tribes abandoned their uncultivated territory, and withdrew beyond the river Gila.

In the year 1517 a navigator from Cuba, Hernandez de Cordova, had while on a cruise discovered an unknown land, which proved to be what is now known as the Peninsula of Yucatan. On his return to Cuba his accounts of the surpassing natural beauty and the untold wealth of the strange land greatly excited the people of that island. The governor, Velasquez, with an ardent purpose of seeking advantage from the discovery, fitted out a squadron of four vessels, which he placed under the command of his nephew, Juan de Grijalva, and dispatched it to the westward. Leaving Cuba on the first day of May, 1518, Grijalva first touched at Cozumel, an island off the coast of Yucatan, and finally sailed as far north as the mouth of the River Panuco, when he returned home.

Velasquez, on learning of the rich empire at the West, was enraged at Grijalva for not having established a colony on the newly discovered coast. He resolved to fit out another armament on a scale of sufficient magnitude to effect the conquest of the country. Having solicited authority from Spain for the purpose, he began preparations, and sought a fit person to take command of the expedition, who at the same time would be able to bear a share of the expense. He decided to give the command to Hernando Cortez, a native of the province of Estremadura, in Spain, who at an early age had sought that field of adventure in the New World which was not open to him in the Old. He had led a wild and reckless life in Hispaniola and Cuba; and at one time, having been detected in a conspiracy against the Government, he was arrested and narrowly escaped with his life. He afterwards engaged in agricultural enterprises and accumulated a competency.

On the eighteenth day of February, 1519,

and at the age of thirty-three or thirty-four, he set sail from Cape San Antonio, in command of an expedition which was to occupy the new land of wonders, and to plant the cross upon its golden shores.

Touching at several intermediate points, he finally landed near San Juan de Ulloa, and, erecting a cross, founded *La Villa Rica de la Vera Cruz*—The Rich City of the True Cross. He was accompanied by five hundred and fifty-three soldiers, sixteen of whom were cavalrymen; and besides these he had one hundred and ten mariners and two hundred Cuban natives.

Having ordered his ships to be sunk, on the pretence that they were unseaworthy, but really to remove from his followers the hope of returning to Cuba, he advanced to the table-lands of the interior, with the intention of conquering the country, of whose wealth he had heard from the Indians of the coast. Having craftily secured the assistance of several tribes hostile to the Aztec dynasty, he marched rapidly across the great central table-land until his progress was opposed by the fierce and warlike Tlascalans. When the news of the approach of the Spaniards was brought to their capital, a council of the leaders was at once convened. An aged chief called Xicotencatl, who is said to have been more than one hundred years old, proposed that his son, who was in command of the armies of Tlascala, should immediately attack the white men, and if defeated, that the council should declare that he had acted without orders. This advice prevailed, and several desperate engagements took place, with unvarying success to the Spanish arms. At last, recognizing the superiority of their adversaries, the Tlascalans implored peace, and offered their assistance in a campaign against their hereditary enemies, the Aztecs. Continuing his march, in company with his new allies, Cortez proceeded to Cholula, the inhabitants of which he massacred without pity or remorse, under the pretence that they contemplated treachery. Then, climbing the mountain-wall, he marched between the volcanoes of Popocatepetl and Iztaccihuatl, and descending into the valley of Tenochtitlan, entered the

Aztec capital, on the eighth day of November, 1519. He was met at the gate by the emperor, the great Montezuma II.

The Spaniards, as they passed over the great dike which extends across the salt flood of Tezcuco, had occasion to observe the mechanical ingenuity displayed by the Aztecs in its construction, as well as in that of the various suburbs, which were built on piles, after the manner of the lake-dwellers of ancient Switzerland. The appearance of the crowded and thriving population of the great city far surpassed everything which the Spaniards had yet seen or conceived. At the Fort of Xoloc, several hundred Aztec chiefs, richly dressed and decorated with a profusion of ornaments, met them to announce the approach of their sovereign. After crossing the drawbridge the retinue of the king came in sight, and the royal palanquin, borne on the shoulders of noblemen, approached. Montezuma descending, walked under a canopy, the ground being covered with cotton tapestry, to receive his unwelcome guests. He wore a cloak of the finest cotton, and sandals the soles of which were of solid gold. Both cloak and sandals sparkled with pearls and precious stones. On his head he wore a panache of *quetzal* feathers. The invaders had found a magnificence and civilization not surpassed in their own country. The architecture of the chief edifices was of a high grade. The manufactures were numerous and diversified. The Aztec goldsmiths exhibited a skill in no respect inferior to that of their fellow-artisans in Europe. The houses were built on foundations of stone; the streets were paved with cement, and intersected by numerous canals. Water was supplied by an earthern main from the neighboring hill of Chapultepec.

Montezuma had transported the Calendar stone, fifty tons in weight, from its native bed of basalt, a distance of many leagues, and had set it up in his own capital. He encouraged art among his nobles, and he himself contributed liberally toward the embellishment of his capital, in which an aviary, a zoölogical garden, and a botanical garden were maintained at great cost. The libraries of the Aztecs contained many thousands of volumes, ingeniously bound, which the Spaniards afterward remorselessly consigned to the flames.

The ostensibly friendly relations between the Aztecs and their visitors were of brief duration; but with the primitive weapons, the arrows, stones, and missiles of one party, and the superior methods of warfare of the other, a contest for supremacy could eventually have but one termination. Still, the struggle was a long and bitter one, and Cortez had many difficulties and reverses to surmount. At the moment of his departure from Cuba, Velasquez, actuated by jealousy, had resolved to deprive him of his command. Learning of the Governor's intention, Cortez sailed away in the night from St. Jago, the gubernatorial seat, and completed his outfit at other ports. In the month of March, 1520, Velasquez sent out an expedition with nine hundred men, under the command of Panfilo de Narvaez, with orders to at once proceed to the new empire, and bring back Cortez as a captive. No sooner had Cortez heard of the arrival of this expedition, and its object, than he sent an envoy to Narvaez, with instructions to propitiate the commander, and at the same time to create a spirit of disaffection among his soldiers by the distribution of gold. Leaving his trusted lieutenant, Pedro de Alvarado, in charge of the capital, Cortez, with two hundred men, surprised Narvaez on a tempestuous night, completely routed him, and, strange to say, succeeded in enlisting his soldiers in his own army, when he returned in triumph to the City of Mexico. Here he was destined to meet with severe reverses, until at length he was forced to withdraw his troops. The night on which this disastrous retreat took place has ever since borne the name of *Noche Triste*, or Melancholy Night. An immense tree is still standing in one of the suburbs of the city, under which Cortez is said to have seated himself and wept over his misfortunes.

Fortunately for the Spaniards, several ships arrived about this time at Vera Cruz, and their crews with little difficulty were induced to join the army of the invader. Observing the improved fortunes of Cortez, all the tribes hostile to the Aztecs now offered him their assistance. The city was besieged and succumbed to an assault on the thirteenth day of August, 1521. The power of the sovereigns of Spain was now firmly established on the soil of the New World.

From this time until 1821, a period of exactly three hundred years, the country remained a province of Spain. With the exception of the first few years of this period it was governed by viceroys, who drained its resources to the lowest ebb.

In honorable contrast with the rest of this long line of vampires, stands the name of Antonio de Bucareli, who governed the country with humanity, and instituted many public improvements.

At last, unable to bear longer the terrible oppression, an insurrectionary spirit began to manifest itself. Finally, at midnight on the fifteenth of September, 1810, Miguel Hidalgo y Costilla, a venerable Roman Catholic priest of the parish of Dolores, in the State of Guanajuato, having called together his people, addressed them from the window of his house and proclaimed the independence of Mexico. The country, ripe for revolt against the hated foreign viceroys, at once rose in arms. A long and sanguinary contest ensued. Hidalgo was at length taken prisoner, while endeavoring to make his way to the United States to procure arms and ammunition, after the rout of his forces at the battle of Puente de Calderon. He was taken to Chihuahua and there shot, on the twenty-seventh of July, 1811. Thus perished the man whose disinterested and patriotic services justly entitle him to be styled "The Washington of Mexico." The grateful remembrance in which his devotion to the holy cause of liberty is held by his countrymen is manifested by the circumstance that there is scarcely a town of any importance that has not erected its monument to his memory. Some of these are very imposing. Mexican art, however, has represented Hidalgo under widely different aspects. In Toluca, a splendid marble statue in the plaza gives the idea of a giant in size, and of commanding presence. On the other hand, a painting in the Hall of the Ambassadors, at the Capital, represents him as a slight, delicate and hollow-chested man, of careworn appearance and apparently studious habit, attired in his priestly garb, having just arisen from his chair, holding in his hand the scroll proclaiming independence, which he is about to read to the people. A colossal bronze statue in the city of San Luis Potosi corresponds closely with the painting, which is in accordance with the universal belief.

After the death of Hidalgo, the revolution was carried on under the leadership of José Maria Morelos, also a Roman Catholic priest. The struggle continued, without any decided success on either side, until the year 1821, when Augustin de Iturbide, a soldier of fortune, born of Spanish parents in the city of Morelia, offered his sword to the insurgents. During the early years of the war, he had shown great zeal in fighting against the patriots, but now he openly espoused their cause. His labors resulted in the triumph of the revolution and the establishment of Mexican independence.

Had Iturbide been less ambitious, his name

would doubtless have taken its place in history with that of the illustrious patriot Hidalgo. But, inflamed by an unbridled ambition, he aspired to absolute power. He was accordingly proclaimed Emperor by his partisans, on the eighteenth day of May, 1822. Three days later he caused Congress to ratify this procedure, and he was duly crowned on the twenty-first of July in the same year.

The people, however, had not rid themselves of one oppressor merely to submit to another. The republican party was very powerful, and on the second of December, Santa Anna, its most distinguished and trusted leader, issued a manifesto proclaiming the Republic, annulling Iturbide's election as emperor, and declaring him an outlaw. The movement was successful. Iturbide was deposed, and on the eleventh of May ensuing he left the country and sailed for Europe, where he remained for more than a year. In the hope that by some possibility he might regain his crown, he returned to Mexico, and arrived at Padilla on the fourteenth of July, 1824. He was at once arrested, and five days later he was taken out and shot.

In 1823 Spain made a futile attempt to retake the country. This was the occasion of the declaration in the seventh annual Message of President Monroe, transmitted to Congress on December 2d, 1823, which in effect forbids the colonization or invasion of this continent by any European power in the future, and which has since become familiarly known as the " Monroe doctrine." It reads as follows :

* * * * The citizens of the United States cherish sentiments the most friendly in favor of the liberty and happiness of their fellow-men on that side of the Atlantic. In the wars of the European powers, in matters relating to themselves, we have never taken any part, nor does it comport with our policy to do so. It is only when our rights are invaded or seriously menaced that we resent injuries or make preparations for our defence. With the movements in this hemisphere we are of necessity more immediately concerned, and by causes which must be obvious to all enlightened and impartial observers. The political system of the allied powers is essentially different in this respect from that of America. This difference proceeds from that which exists in their respective governments. And to the defence of our own, which has been achieved by the loss of so much blood and treasure, and matured by the wisdom of their most enlightened citizens, and under which we have enjoyed unexampled felicity, this whole nation is devoted. We owe it, therefore, to candor and to the amicable relations existing between the United States and those powers, to declare that we should consider any attempt on their part to extend their system to any portion of this hemisphere as dangerous to our peace and safety. With the existing colonies or dependencies of any European power we have not interfered, and shall not interfere. But with the governments who have declared their independence, we have, on great consideration and on just principles, acknowledged we could not view any interposition for the purpose of oppressing them, or controlling in any other manner their destiny, by any European power, in any other light than as the manifestation of an unfriendly disposition towards the United States.

A republican form of government was now firmly established. The next event of importance was the war with the United States; but as the reputation of our country for honor and fair dealing was not increased by the circumstances which led to it, it may be well to pass over its history.

The religious and political history of Mexico from the date of the Spanish conquest down to the year 1867 have been so intimately blended that it is hardly an exaggeration to say that they have been one and the same. The Roman

Catholic worship, established by Cortez on the ruins of the ancient superstitions, existed unchallenged for over three centuries. The first Mexican Constitution, adopted in 1824, contained these words: " The religion of the Mexican nation is, and will be perpetually, the Roman Catholic Apostolic. The nation will protect it by wise and just laws, and prohibit the exercise of any other whatever." Under this new stimulus the Church continued to grow in power and importance, so that it soon dominated everything, political, social, and even domestic. The number of religious houses was enormous. The officials of the Church had the complete monopoly even of banking and other financial matters. They acknowledged possessions amounting to one hundred and eighty million dollars, but probably three hundred millions would be nearer the truth. Some writers have estimated that their possessions comprised one-third of all the real and personal property in the Republic; and as it was exempt from taxation, the burden on the remaining property of the country was, of course, correspondingly augmented.

In the year 1856 a spirit of opposition to the temporal authority of the Church began to manifest itself. A bitter controversy between the partisans of the old *régime* and the Liberal party before long agitated the whole Republic. General Miramon was the acknowledged leader of the former. He afterwards held high rank in the army of Maximilian, and finally shared his fate.

Under the able leadership of Benito Juarez, a pure-blooded Indian, born in the State of Oaxaca, the Liberal party triumphed, and the present constitution, curtailing the power of the Church, was promulgated on the fifth of February, 1857. The utmost energy of the government was now put forth to assure the subordination of the religious to the civil power. New laws and regulations were established, many of which were severe, not to say oppressive. In some of the States the bells cannot be rung without the special permission of the authorities, and priests are not suffered even to walk the streets in their clerical gowns.

Among the most striking evidences of the decadence of the power of the Church which impress a stranger, is the number of abandoned and ruined church edifices with which he everywhere meets. Some of them are occupied as military barracks and others are used for business and other secular purposes. One of the finest churches in Vera Cruz has been converted into a store-house for sugar, and another at Orizaba, as has been already remarked, is used as a ring for the bull-fights. It remains, however, to be added, that in some of the States the influence of the Roman Church is still very powerful.

During the administration of President Juarez, the Mexican Congress, in June, 1861, passed a law confiscating ecclesiastical property. On the seventeenth of July following, Congress passed another measure which was productive of great and momentous results. It provided for " a suspension for two years of payments on account of the foreign debt and of all national liability." A portion of the foreign debt was owing to England, France and Spain. These powers at once formed an alliance for securing themselves against loss, and each agreed to furnish troops, to make up an army, which was to proceed to Mexico, accompanied by commissioners, for the purpose of securing the payment of their respective debts. Accordingly an army of ten thousand men was landed at Vera Cruz, on the tenth of January, 1862.

It was not long before the commissioners of England and Spain discovered that Napoleon III. had sent his forces to Mexico for the real purpose of establishing an imperial government on the Western Continent, and that he had only used the matter of the debt as a pretext for his invasion. They consequently withdrew.

It has been asserted that the purpose of the French tyrant and usurper was to treat with our Southern States then in rebellion, and with them to form a vast slave empire, which should control the cotton-growing region of the North American Continent. He sent a large army to Mexico, which in due time made its way by force of arms to the capital. The throne of the newly erected Mexican Empire was then offered, for political reasons, to the Archduke Maximilian of Austria. He accepted the proffered crown, and arrived in Mexico on the twenty-ninth of May, 1864. He was strenuously opposed by the adherents of the Liberal party and by the mass of the Mexican people. Still, he received a certain support from a faction which, in the expected triumph of Maximilian, coming as he did with the papal blessing, hoped to see the supremacy of the Church re-established. On the other hand, all those who had purchased its confiscated estates sided with the Liberals, as in the event of Maximilian's success they feared that these would be wrested from them and restored to the Church.

Owing to the civil war in the United States we had been powerless to prevent this flagrant violation of the terms of the " Monroe doctrine." But on the cessation of hostilities, General U. S. Grant, with the co-operation of the Secretary of State, William H. Seward, and the approval of President Johnson, ordered General Sheridan, with an army of seventy thousand veterans, to proceed to the Rio Grande del Norte. The Emperor of the French was now notified by a cable telegram that his armies must be immediately withdrawn from the soil of Mexico.

The terms of this peremptory and humiliating demand were of course promptly complied with. The unfortunate Maximilian, not having the sagacity to return with the French army to Europe, soon found himself surrounded by enemies on every side. His army was reduced to the small Austrian contingent which had accompanied him, and such Mexican troops as still remained true to him. Leaving the beautiful palace of Chapultepec he withdrew to the city of Queretaro, and there surrendered to the Liberal forces under General Escobedo, on the fourteenth of May, 1867.

He was subsequently tried by court-martial and condemned to death, the same sentence being pronounced upon his two generals, Miramon and Mejia. He died as he came, a freebooter on the soil of Mexico.

Maximilian probably would have been forgiven his political offences, at least his life would have been spared, if, prompted by the infamous Bazaine, he had not in a weak moment signed an order declaring that all Mexicans taken prisoners with arms in their hands should be condemned to death and their sentence executed within twenty-four hours. Pursuant to this order many patriots were butchered in cold blood. Every effort was made by his friends to save his life, but without avail. Even Secretary Seward intimated a wish to President Juarez that his life might be spared, but he received the pertinent reply that the United States was great enough and powerful enough to be generous; but not so with Mexico.

On the nineteenth day of June, 1867, Maximilian was marched out to the foot of the Cerro de las Campanas, a small hill near Queretaro, and was there shot—his generals Miramon and Mejia falling at the same moment. The story which has been circulated by some penny-a-liner that he uttered with his dying breath the words "Poor Carlotta!" is undoubtedly destitute of all foundation. As he received the volley of the firing party he ejaculated, in his native tongue, what in English is equivalent to the exclamation "Oh my!" and that was all.

His body was embalmed, and it now reposes in the imperial vault at Vienna.

On the night preceding his execution he addressed the following letter to his wife. It is probably the most creditable act of his life.

"To my beloved Charlotte:

"If God ever permits you to recover and read these lines, you will learn the cruelty of the fate which has not ceased to pursue me since your departure for Europe. You carried with you my soul and my happiness. Why did I not listen to you? So many events, alas! so many unexpected and unmerited catastrophes, have overwhelmed me, that I have no more hope in my heart, and I await death as a delivering angel. I die without agony. I shall fall with glory, like a soldier, like a conquered king. If you have not the power to bear so much suffering, if God soon reunites us, I shall bless the divine and paternal Hand which has so rudely stricken us. Adieu! Adieu.

"Thy poor Max."

What precise share his nearest blood relations

of the imperial House of Hapsburg had in the atrocious conspiracy which was originally hatched by the villain who had trampled under foot the free constitution of France, will probably never be known until the deep shall give up its dead. That they felt relieved by the formal relinquishment of his possible claim to the crown of Austria, which they exacted, there is abundant evidence. If the truth shall ever come to light, it may be found that they secretly exulted in his miserable doom.

Let us hope that this episode in the annals of our sister republic will serve as a bloody buoy, warning the despots of Europe, in all coming time, to keep aloof from the republics of America.

CHAPTER V.

THE CITY OF MEXICO.

The City of Mexico is situated in the middle of a large basin which was anciently covered by the waters of Lake Tezcuco. Hence, while it is seven thousand three hundred and fifty feet above the level of the sea, it nevertheless stands on ground considerably lower than the surrounding region. Even in the dry season, the winter, when the water of the lake is at the lowest, it is only six feet below the grade of the city. The obstacles to thorough drainage have not yet been surmounted, and accordingly Mexico cannot be considered a healthy place of residence. During the rainy season the contents of the sewers are constantly more or less disturbed, which, of course, renders the atmosphere impure.

Pre-eminent among the writers who have described the natural features of Mexico stands the name of the illustrious Humboldt. Whoever desires accurately to inform himself regarding the geology, topography and physical geography of that country may wisely addict himself to the study of the records made by that eminent explorer in the year 1804. It may indeed be doubted whether any succeeding writer has added anything of value to his discoveries and observations. Accordingly, it is to me a source of unalloyed satisfaction to remember that the noble bust of Humboldt looks benignly upon every visitor who enters the Central Park from Fifth Avenue. I may add that, on my homeward journey through the city of St. Louis, I was both surprised and delighted to find an imposing statue of bronze, commemorative of that great man, occupying the most conspicuous place in the beautiful pleasure-ground which bears the name of Tower Grove Park.

The description given by him of the site of the City of Mexico in every particular corresponds with what may be stated to-day. The Mexico rebuilt by Cortez, he informs us, is smaller than Tenochtitlan under the last of the

Montezumas. What gives the newer city a peculiar and distinctive character is the fact that it is situated entirely on the continent, between the extremities of the two lakes of Tezcuco and Xochimilco, and that it only receives, by means of navigable canals, the fresh water of the Xochimilco. There are five of these lakes in the valley of Mexico, four of which are salt. The largest of these, Lake Tezcuco, is the highest body of salt water known to exist on the globe. Cortez described it as an interior sea, whose tides continually ebbed and flowed. The action of the winds probably occasioned his mistake in this regard. The water is more salt than that of the Baltic Sea, but less so than that of the ocean. Sulphide of hydrogen is exhaled in great quantities from all these lakes, and undoubtedly adds at certain seasons to the insalubrity of the valley. Humboldt, however, remarks as a curious fact that intermittent fevers are of rare occurrence.

Nevertheless, strangers taking up their residence in the City of Mexico, until they have become acclimated are liable to suffer from a mild form of fever, and caution should accordingly be exercised to avoid taking cold. This, however, is no easy matter. The doors and windows of the houses are not well fitted, and of course the inmates are often exposed to draughts of cold air. Even in the palaces and more costly residences there are no stoves, fire-places or appliances of any kind for warming the apartments. A Mexican will tell you that fire attenuates the atmosphere, and this is not conducive to health. It is indeed true that individuals who have lived on the sea-coast cannot at once accommodate themselves to the rarefied atmosphere of the Mexican capital. Hence, it is customary with such, when circumstances admit of it, to sojourn temporarily at a place of intermediate altitude, like Orizaba.

The population of the City of Mexico is variously estimated from two hundred and twenty-five thousand to two hundred and seventy-five thousand souls. No enumeration of the inhabitants has ever been made, hence the discrepancy referred to.

The hotels are kept on the European plan.

You engage a room, or a suite of rooms, at a stated price, and take your meals wherever you please. The prices here are higher than at any other place in the country, the cost of moderate living being about four dollars a day. The best restaurants are conducted by foreigners. They are not fitted up with much elegance, but the quality of the fare is excellent. Better than all, you here escape the everlasting grease and spice that characterize the ordinary Mexican cookery. Corned beef swimming in oil, and rice saturated with lard and seasoned with red pepper may, however, be very palatable for those whose taste runs that way. The French arrangement of meals is adopted throughout the country,—a refection of coffee and rolls in the morning, breakfast in the middle of the day and dinner in the evening.

The Hotel Iturbide is the principal hotel in the city, and is the favorite resort of Americans. It was originally designed as a palace for the Emperor Iturbide; but before it was completed he had met his fate at the hands of the executioner.

The hackney-coaches are of three several classes, and are distinguished from each other by flags of different colors attached to the driver's seat. The prices are graded accordingly. For those carrying blue flags, the rate is one dollar per hour; for those carrying red flags, seventy-five cents; and for those carrying white flags, fifty cents. These prices are doubled after ten o'clock in the evening. The driver takes down his flag the moment that the services of his vehicle are engaged; and the customer is required to pay for its use from the time of engaging till the return to the spot where he originally engaged it.

There is also a very complete system of street railroads. The cars are designated as first-class and second-class, and mules are employed to draw them. The regulations do not appear to be very strict. I have seen passengers bring live hogs on board the second-class cars. There are two conductors to each car, one who sells tickets to passengers and the other who collects them. Each in this way serves as a check on the other. Wages, however, must be low, and laborers numerous, if the companies can afford to employ so many men. On a few lines the American bell-punch is used.

The foreign residents, including the Ambassadors and their *attachés*, the railroad projectors, and the English, French and German store-keepers, constitute quite a colony by themselves. The Americans have a club-house and grounds at La Piedad, several miles distant from the city. The English and French languages are in general use among the better educated class of the population. As though preparing for the next phase of their history as a people, everybody seems to be learning to speak English.

The variety of costumes to be seen on the street is wonderful. The ladies are beginning to adopt the fashions of Paris. Still, many adhere to the old Spanish style of lace on the head, black mantillas, rather short skirts, and high-heeled shoes, the style so well delineated in the pictures of Fortuny, Boldini, Madrazo and others. Indeed, I think that artists who are in the practice of choosing Oriental scenes in order to introduce coloring into their work, may turn their attention to Mexico with advantage. They will find there the richest flesh-tints, and costumes of every variety of color.

As for the men's apparel, with the exception of a small number of the upper class, who adopt the French fashions, there seems to be no prescribed style of dress, except an immense hat and a short jacket for those who choose to wear it, instead of a shawl. Both in the city and in the country you not unfrequently encounter men whose entire suit is of leather. Fire-arms are everywhere carried in plain sight. The Mexican especially affects a handsome revolver with an ivory handle. Horsemen frequently carry a sword, not suspended from the waist in military fashion, but fastened to the saddle. Throughout the rural districts the men carry a large heavy knife, called the *machete*, with a blade about two feet long and two and a half inches wide. While it is made in New England, and is extensively used in the Spanish West India Islands, it may, very properly, be called the National Knife of Mexico. There it is used for an almost infinite variety of purposes. It not only enables the agricultural laborer to cut down the sugar-cane, and even trees of moderate size, but it likewise serves as a formidable weapon of offence and defence.

Sunday is a grand gala day. Everybody goes abroad dressed in the best possible style. A military band plays during the greater part of the day in the Plaza, and there is a general air of bustle and merry-making. The shops of the better and more fashionable description are open till noon; the arcades are thronged by itinerant venders of every variety of wares, some of the articles probably being stolen. These hucksters generally accept half the price at first demanded, and sometimes even much less than that. A bull-fight in the afternoon and a ball in the evening usually complete the enjoyments of the day. The *pulque* is the popular beverage. This is a concoction of the fermented juice of the maguey, and is drunk by everybody. One must practise to like it; otherwise he might imagine it to be the magic draught of witches.

The drives in the environs are very beautiful. The most fashionable of these is the *Pasco*

The City of Mexico.

de la Reforma, one of the avenues of the new park. This was the favorite drive of the unfortunate Empress Carlotta, and is often called "the Mad Woman's Drive." At half-past five in the afternoon the avenue is crowded with the equipages of the foreign Ambassadors, the bankers, merchants and wealthier residents generally. The park is extensive and well kept, its avenues are broad, and at intervals they widen into circles, which are ornamented with statues of King Charles IV. of Spain, Christopher Columbus, and the Goddess of Liberty. One is about to be erected to Benito Juarez, the Deliverer of Mexico.

At the southern extremity of the park stands the Palace of Chapultepec, on the site where formerly stood the imperial abode of Montezuma. It was the residence of the Emperor Maximilian during the greater portion of his brief reign, and is now occupied for military purposes. It is about to be fitted up for the summer abode of the President.

A little further on is the village of Tacubaya, where many residents of the city have tasteful villas. The retreat of Cortez and the Spaniards from Mexico in 1520 was by this route, and the Melancholy Night constitutes an epoch in the early history of New Spain. The tree of *Noche Triste* still commemorates the event, and is pointed out to travellers.

Three miles to the north of the city is the village of Guadalupe with its celebrated church. This edifice was built to commemorate the appearing of the Blessed Virgin to an Indian proselyte named Juan Diego. From the moment of its consecration it became the most distinguished Christian sanctuary in New Spain. The railings, tabernacle, lamps, and other ornaments are of silver. The innumerable votive offerings which cover the walls are so many testimonials to the wonderful cures performed by the Holy Virgin of Guadalupe. When Hidalgo reared the standard of Mexican independence in 1810, her image was painted upon his banner. After the successful establishment of the Republic the place was exalted to civic dignity under the designation of the City of Guadalupe Hidalgo. The treaty of peace between the United States and Mexico in 1848 was signed here by the plenipotentiaries of both countries, and it has ever since been known as *The Treaty of Gaudalupe Hidalgo.*

The shops of Mexico are very fine, and the variety of articles sold is great. It may afford some criterion of the wealth of the people to remark that no very costly goods are offered for sale. The notion generally prevails that American tourists have an unlimited supply of money. Every trader is accordingly on the *qui vive* to turn an honest penny at their expense. The instant that the fact becomes known that you desire an article of a particular kind, such as bric-à-brac or relics, your apartments are besieged by a small army of dealers offering to supply it. If the thing exhibited does not chance to please you, they promise to bring something to-morrow that will certainly suit *El Señor*. Sure enough, they are on hand the next day, with something very near, if not exactly, what is desired. It would be curious, and might be instructive, to know where the article has been procured.

Lotteries are very popular, and you are solicited on every hand to buy a ticket. Some of them are carried on under the auspices of the Government, and even churches are in part supported by them.

One of the most interesting features of the city, which, however, is often neglected by visitors, is the Viga. This is a canal, running along the line of a broad highway. The sides of the road and the banks of the canal are shaded by fine trees, many of them willows and Lombardy poplars. It extends to Lake Chalco, and is used for bringing vegetables and the various country products into the city. It can be reached by street cars. On arriving at the canal I found a flat-boat with a low roof, which, by a little stretch of the imagination, might be assimilated to a Venetian gondola. After I had gone on board, the boatman took his position in the bow and with a pole propelled the craft on its way. The water was only five feet deep, and he was able to get on at a fair rate of speed without much difficulty. These boatmen are generally Indians.

A more picturesque scene can hardly be imagined than is presented here toward the close of the day. I could discern all the objects on the avenue as well as on the water, including the freight and passengers. The working people, most of whom are Indians, were going home from their daily toil. In general, they travelled in a dug-out canoe, like their fellow aborigines of more northern climes. Each man sat in the stern and propelled his craft with a paddle, while his family occupied the bow. High-sounding names were painted on these canoes, many of them being of a religious character.

The municipal police force is large, and under admirable management and discipline. The patrolmen wear a uniform of dark blue cloth, with a military cap of white duck. At night a long cloak, also blue, is added, and they carry lanterns. When they are not walking they place these in the middle of the streets to indicate where they are. It seems to be the practice for them to stand at the corners of the streets, rather than to keep constantly in motion.

The postal regulations are somewhat peculiar,

and I must say they admit of essential improvement. Mexicans evidently do not write many letters, if we may judge from the small number of names on the bulletin-lists at the post-offices. Pursuant to the provisions of the postal treaty, the rate of postage to the United States is six cents, but for any distance within the boundaries of the Republic exceeding seventeen leagues it is twenty-five cents. All postage must be prepaid by stamps, but the arrangements in this respect are clumsy and troublesome. The individual desiring to mail a letter is required to deliver his letter, and at the same time the money, to the clerk at the post-office and he affixes the stamp. The stamps distributed among the several States are numbered, and those belonging to one State may not be used in another. Stamps are not sold to individuals as in this country, except in rare instances at the discretion of the postmaster.

The Cathedral of Mexico is a building of extraordinary beauty and grandeur. Its dimensions far exceed those of every other Christian temple in the Western Hemisphere, and justly entitle it to rank with St. Peter's at Rome, and with the magnificent cathedrals at Milan and Cologne. To those who are familiar with the splendid edifice which stands on Fifth Avenue between Fiftieth and Fifty-first Streets, it is only necessary to say that in size the cathedral at the City of Mexico is nearly twice as great. No person of architectural culture and taste can look upon the grand pile, within or without, and fail to receive an impression which time cannot efface.

It is situated on the Plaza Mayor, and with the Sagrario, it occupies the entire northern side of the square. It was built on the site of the Great Temple of Huitzilopochtli, the war-god of the Aztec race. The work was begun in 1573 and was completed in ninety-four years, having cost the sum of 1,752,000 dollars. The edifice, with the minor structures, is five hundred feet in length by four hundred and twenty feet in width; and its towers are each two hundred feet high. The superb panoramic view from the eastern tower gives the observer an accurate conception of the various districts and localities in the City of Mexico. There are no less than forty-eight bells in these towers, many of which are dedicated to the saints and more distinguished martyrs of the Roman Catholic calendar. Among these are Santa Maria de Guadalupe, thirty-six feet high, Doña Maria, weighing fifteen thousand pounds, and Saint Angel, weighing fourteen thousand pounds. A handsome clock with a gilt dial-plate surmounts the main entrance. Standing near it are the figures of the three Christian Virtues, Faith, Hope and Charity. The cupola is octagonal in form and is almost as high as the towers. It is wrought and adorned with great elegance. The fine painting in fresco, by Junciro, representing the Assumption of the Virgin, constitutes one of the ornaments of the interior.

The cathedral is built after the style of the Spanish Renaissance. It has five naves. On the sides of the two lateral naves are fourteen chapels, enclosed with balustrades of carved wood. There are also six others, namely: the Chapel of the Kings, in which the viceroys were buried; the Chapel of Souls, where the remains of the priests were deposited; the Chapel of Good Resolution, the Chapel of Saint Joseph, the Chapel of Saint Lawrence, and the Chapel of Forgiveness of Sins. In the last of these a mass is said every half hour of the day throughout the entire year.

The main altar, covered by a canopy supported by eight columns, is situated in the centre of the cathedral, between the choir and the altar of the kings. The latter is surrounded by a balustrade which is ornamented by sixty-two figures, each holding a candlestick. A figure representing the Holy Virgin, and also statues of the apostles and principal saints, all of life size, stand about the main altar. These were formerly adorned with precious stones presented by Charles V.

It would, however, require a book to describe this magnificent structure and its decorations as they deserve, and I will attempt it no further.

The celebrated Aztec Calendar Stone leans against the exterior wall of the cathedral. It is circular in form, eleven feet in diameter and three feet thick. It once adorned the Great Aztec Temple, and was probably made in the year 1279. It was carved from a piece of porous basalt, and is covered with hieroglyphics indicating the months of the year. It was found in 1790 buried in the Plaza, which itself formerly constituted a part of the precinct of the Great Temple. Calendars made of gold and silver were highly esteemed by the former rulers of Mexico. Montezuma presented Cortez with two, both richly carved, which are described as being "as large as cart-wheels," one representing the sun and the other the moon. Another of solid gold was found by a soldier, during the sack of Tenochtitlan, in the garden of Guatemozin, the last of the Aztec Emperors. The Aztec sages were as devoted star-gazers as the ancient Chaldeans and had as elaborate an astronomy. The Spaniards, however, were not savants in search of learning, and every fabric of gold or silver, no matter how beautiful or curious, was hurried to the melting-pot. The English have never failed to display a similar rapacity in Hindostan. Warren Hastings, when governor, took much interest in archæology. Finding a deposit of ancient Persian darics he sent them home as curiosities to the East India Company. His zeal was ill-judged; they were speedily melted down for the gold. The Spaniards could hardly have done worse.

The Mexicans take a just pride in their National Gallery of Paintings, the *Academia de San Carlos.* The collection is large, and many of the pictures are after the style of the old masters. Those of the modern school, in which department native talent is well represented, possess decided merit.

The College of Mines is a well-regulated institution. It was built by Don Manuel Tolsa seventy years ago at a cost of one and a half million dollars, and covers an area of about two acres. Its organization as a school of science is very complete, and it deserves the careful attention of the tourist.

The building in which the Inquisition of Mexico formerly held its dread convocations is now occupied by the National School of Medicine.

The new building of the National Library is perhaps the finest edifice in the city.

The *Palacio del Gobierno,* or Government Palace, is also situated upon the Plaza. It is six hundred and seventy-five feet long and two stories high. It was commenced by Cortez, and for three centuries was occupied as the vice-regal residence. Since the establishment of Mexican independence it has been used by the Government for public affairs, including the Post Office, the military barracks and the National Museum.

The Hall of the Ambassadors, the principal room in the Palace, is a handsome and spacious apartment, being three hundred feet long and twenty-five feet wide. It is opened only on special occasions. I had the opportunity of seeing it, through the courtesy of the Governor of the Palace. The walls are hung with the portraits of the heroes and great men of Mexico, Hidalgo, Morelos, Iturbide, Juarez and others. A single foreigner only has been admitted to this Pantheon,—Washington. There is a picture of the battle of Puebla, in which the French were defeated by the Mexican forces. With a pardonable patriotism, the artist has depicted the enemy in headlong flight and the field covered with their dead.

I paid numerous visits to the National Museum and took the greatest interest in the collections. Here are preserved old Spanish arms, glassware that had belonged to the Emperor Iturbide, the silver table-service and medals of Maximilian; also his state carriage, which was made in the most expensive fashion after the style of such carriages in Europe.

There is a very complete collection of Aztec and pre-Aztec antiquities. The most notable of these, the Sacrificial Stone, was cut from a huge block of jasper, and is about equal in its dimensions to the Calendar Stone, which I have already described. In the centre is a bowl-shaped depression, evidently for the purpose of receiving the blood of the victim, which was carried off by a groove or trough extending to the edge. The mode of slaughter consisted in stretching the wretched victim upon the surface of the stone, five priests holding fast his head and limbs, while the sixth, with a razor of volcanic glass or obsidian, opened his breast, and thrusting in one hand tore out the heart. He first held it up to the sun, and then placed it on a censer at the feet of the statue of Huitzilopotchli, around which was the coiled figure of the Sacred Rattlesnake. This abominable rite seems to have belonged peculiarly to the Aztecs. The older race of Toltecs are generally represented as making bloodless offerings. Human sacrifices dated back only about two centuries before the Spanish Conquest. There were many of these sacrificial stones, not only in Tenochtitlan but in the other cities of the Aztec dominion; and the number put to death seems almost incredible. It is stated by Father Torquemada that at the dedication of the Great Temple, or Hall of Serpents, in 1486, a procession of prisoners two miles long and numbering seventy-two thousand perished on the very stone which I have described.

There is a very extensive collection of Aztec idols in this museum. They are for the most part grotesque and fantastic in appearance.

Many of the figures are those of animals; but the rattlesnake is the most common symbol.

The serpent-worship will be described in the next chapter.

CHAPTER VI.

THE SERPENT-WORSHIP.

On the eve of my departure for Mexico, my learned and greatly valued friend, Dr. Alexander Wilder, did me the honor to present me with a copy of his curious and interesting monograph on THE SERPENT-WORSHIP. At the same time he paid me the compliment to remark he would feel under obligation for any information which I might communicate to him, on my return, concerning the serpent-cultus of the ancient Mexicans; to the end that he might embody it in his more elaborate work, to be entitled "Serpent and Siva Worship," which is now in the course of preparation for the press.

With my attention thus directed to the subject, I have availed myself of every opportunity which has offered to study the general subject, to collect images and to make sketches of such

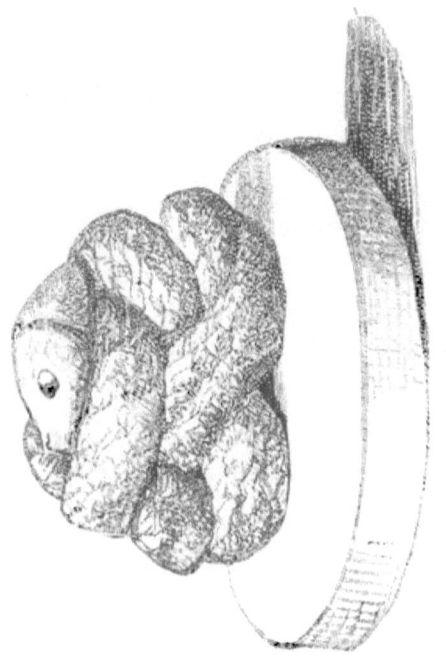

SACRED SERPENT.

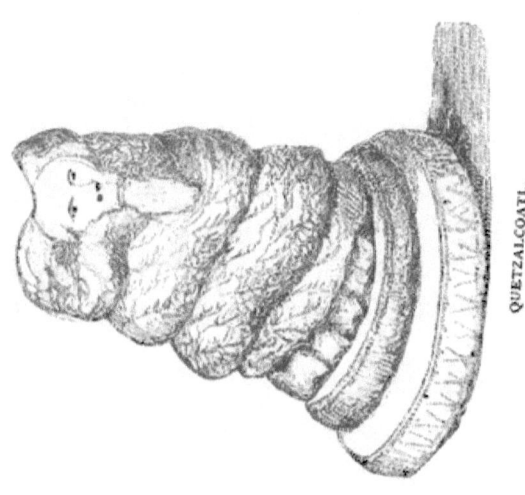

QUETZALCOATL.

of the veritable idols of the Toltec and Aztec worship as have come in my way. The representations of the Serpent-gods of Mexico, carved in stone, were generally destroyed by the Spaniards. The *simulacra* of several of them are, however, preserved in the National Museum. The general form is that of a coiled serpent. I annex copies of a pencil sketch of two of these images, which I made during one of my visits to the National Museum.

Mr. Bradford, in his work on American Antiquities, describes the image of the goddess Teoyaomiqui,—which is preserved in the University of Mexico—as a statue of colossal dimensions and terrible form. A traveller has described it as hewn out of a solid block of basalt, nine feet high. Its outlines, we are told, are a combination of a deformed human figure with all that is horrible in the tiger and the rattle-snake. Instead of arms, it is supplied with two large serpents; while its drapery is composed of wreathed snakes interwoven in the most disgusting manner, and the sides terminate in the wings of a vulture. Its feet are those of a tiger, and between them lies the head of a rattlesnake, which seems to be descending from the body of the idol. Humboldt says: "The arms and feet were hidden under a drapery, surrounded by enormous serpents, which the Mexicans denoted by the name of *cohuatlicuye*, garment of serpents."

The accompanying effigy, cut from a carefully executed photograph, represents this idol.

In Mexico, as in every other portion of the western hemisphere where the serpent was found in nature, it appears to have been a universal symbol of divinity. In the ancient picture-writing, carved upon walls, and coiled around idols, the mystic figure was everywhere to be seen, reminding us of a faith and worship that to many will seem incredible. If we may credit the account of Bernal Diaz, the historiographer of the Spanish Conquest, living rattlesnakes were maintained in the Great Temple, or, as it was then called, the Hall of Serpents, at Mexico, as sacred or petted objects. They were kept in a cabin, in which a quantity of feathers had been strewn. There they laid their eggs and reared

THE GODDESS TEOYAOMIQUI.

their young. They were fed indiscriminately with the remains of human sacrifices and with dogs'-meat. He also tells us that the Spaniards, in their march under Cortez to Mexico, came to a place called Terraguca, which, on account of the numerous figures of these reptiles found in the temples, where they were worshipped by the natives as gods, they named *The Town of Serpents*.

This worship would appear to be in close analogy to the practices of the races inhabiting the Ancient World. The apocryphal Book of Daniel, as printed in the Bibles of other days, relates the story of a dragon which the Babylonians worshipped; and the Book of Kings declares that Hezekiah broke in pieces the brazen serpent made by Moses, because it was an object of idolatry among the Israelites. In the temples of Egypt figures of the serpent were everywhere to be met with; and living serpents were maintained in the Grecian sanctuaries of Apollo and Esculapius. The consecration of a new shrine of these divinities was accompanied by the transportation thither of one of these reptiles from a parent temple. At the present time living snakes are worshipped in parts of Hindostan and of Africa. In contrast with the asp of Egypt, the colubers of Europe and the *cobra de capello* of India, the rattlesnake enjoys the distinction of being the sacred emblem of America.

The wall which surrounded the site of the Great Temple of Mexico was denominated *Coatepantli*, the Wall of Serpents. Humboldt relates that the triangular roof of the temple of Quetzalcoatl was surrounded by one of these symbolical figures. One of the titles of this divinity was Yolcohuatl, the rattlesnake; and the entrance to his sanctuary in Mexico represented the jaws of an immense serpent. The place of his disappearance was denominated *Coatzacoalco*, the hiding-place of the rattlesnake; and he was fabled to have taken his departure from Mexico in a boat of serpent-skins.

A favorite designation of the rattlesnake among the various native tribes of North America, by whom it was frequently identified with the sun, was The Great Father. The rattlesnake was also adored as the parent of mankind. Such was the belief of the ancient Peruvians.

The Supreme Divinity of the Mexicans was Tonacatlcoatl, the Genius, or, more literally, the Serpent, of the Sun. His consort was designated indifferently Cihuacohuatl and Tonacacihua, the Wife of the Serpent, or the Spouse of the Sun. A tradition existed similar to that of the Peruvians, that they became parents of twins, a son and a daughter, from whom descended all mankind. Hence the invocation of the Aztec litany: "We entreat that those who die in war may be received by thee, our Father, the Sun, and our brother the earth; for thou alone reignest."

This belief has its parallel in the mythological legends of the ancient world. The Scythians, according to Herodotus, ascribed their origin to Echidna, the Serpent-woman, and Hercules, the Moloch or Sun-god of Western Asia. Traditions of the Armenians, Asiatics, Ethiopians and Abyssinians, ascribe to their kings a descent from Zohak, the murderous snake of the Avesta; and the Naga tribes of Kashmir and India trace a similar lineage. Even the Athenian Cecrops was depicted with ophidian extremities, and the mother of Alexander the Great pretended that he was the offspring of the Bacchic Serpent.

I see little difference between the serpent-worship of the East and that of America. In each is the same reference to an original father, an era of prosperity, and an intimate relation with natural events. The serpent not only typifies the first parent, but the sun and the lightning. In India it is the withholder of rain, in China and Mexico it forms the clouds and causes the rain to fall. It dispenses benefits and is the great benefactor of mankind.

Quetzalcoatl, the son or incarnation of Tonacatlcoatl, the all-sustaining god, is sometimes represented by the figure of a rattlesnake with *quetzal* feathers. But alone of all the gods of the Aztecs he is commonly depicted as having a human body.

Some writers have suggested a method of interpretation whereby the various supernatural myths, fairy tales and religious traditions are all explained as relating to solar and meteorological occurrences. According to this hypothesis, the legends of Quetzalcoatl are so many sun-myths. His advent from the Far East, or Tlapallan, his accession to supreme power, and his final departure with a promise to return from the East and renew his reign with augmented splendor, would thus become a symbolical representation of the King of Day at the various stages of dawn, noonday and decadence.

Many of the characteristics ascribed to Quetzalcoatl are consonant with such an explanation. The morning star was his symbol, and the Teocalli at Cholula was dedicated to him as the author of light. He was accordingly characterized as the inventor of the calendar, because he was the creator of days. Like Viracocha of the Peruvians and other divinities of the dawn, he was represented as of fair complexion, clad in white or shining robes and wearing a full beard.

The historian Prescott describes him somewhat differently as he appeared in the Teocalli of Cholula. "On the summit," says he, "stood a sumptuous temple, in which was the image of the mystic deity, 'God of the Air,' with ebon features, unlike the fair complexion which he bore upon earth, wearing a mitre upon his head waving with plumes of fire, with a resplendent collar of gold round his neck, pendants of mosaic turquoise in his ears, a jewelled sceptre in one hand, and a shield curiously painted, the emblem of his rule over the winds, in the other."

The hieroglyphical symbol by which Quetzalcoatl is denoted, *a feathered rattlesnake*, was undoubtedly a homophone of his name, the *quetzal* being a kind of paroquet and *cohuatl*, the Aztec word for snake. This has everywhere been a common device of occult symbolism. The bird represented the wind and the serpent denoted the lightning. Quetzalcoatl or Kukulkan was therefore the lord of the storm and the lightning. He appears to have been the counterpart of Rimmon, of ancient Assyria, who was also the god of the wind; and in accordance with the same analogy, as air is in a manner identical with health, life and spirit. He was also the lord of intelligence, wisdom and prophetic intuition. Like Prometheus of the old

Hellenic mythology he gave fire to men, and peace, plenty and every earthly blessing were diffused among his subjects. He was the ideal of goodness, and is represented as of majestic stature and dignified demeanor. Artificers and men of learning came with him. "He was chaste and temperate in life," declares Brasseur de Bourbourg, "wise in council, generous in gifts, conquering by the arts of peace rather than by those of war; delighting in music, flowers and brilliant colors. So averse was he to human sacrifices that he shut his ears with both hands when they were mentioned."

If it is asked how these characteristics are reconcilable with the atrocious rites employed in his worship, it may be answered that history abounds with examples where divinities, whose attributes were peaceful and merciful, were worshipped with ceremonies of an opposite character. The Aztecs were not originally the worshippers of Quetzalcoatl. He was a god of the Mayas, Toltecs and Nahuas, who worshipped him with milder and more humane rites. The Aztecs, when they adopted him, made him the son of

Mexcoatl, on whose sacrificial stones human victims were mercilessly slaughtered.

Human sacrifices seem to have been a universal characteristic of the worship of the serpent. The ancient Israelites during the period that they burned incense to the Brazen Serpent of Moses " slew their children in sacrifice, used secret ceremonies, and made revellings of strange rites." The Greeks at the Bacchic orgies and the festivals of Poseidon put men to death, till after the Doric and Hellenic revolution, attribbuted by the myth-writers to Hercules and Theseus. The Phœnicians and Carthaginians were notorious for kidnapping women and children for the services of their gods and for the numbers of human victims whom they immolated. The Romans, Egyptians and other Eastern nations perpetrated like enormities. Several of the snake-worshipping tribes of Africa sacrifice human victims to their idols at the present day.

Mr. Fergusson has ingeniously conjectured that the reign of Quetzalcoatl was somewhere between the sixth and ninth century of our era, and synchronous with a corresponding time of prosperity in Cambodia and Farther India. Although Buddhism at the beginning superseded the serpent-worship and bloody sacrifices, the Naga-religion was afterward engrafted upon it in Northern India. Hence the sculptures and architectural remains at Cambodia as well as at Sanchi and Amaravati exhibit the ophite worship in full splendor. Whether the simultaneous prevalence of the serpent-cultus in Eastern Asia and its appearance in America are evidence of propagandism is a matter for curious enquiry. It is certain that Buddhism and its kindred faith Jainism dispensed with all cruel and bloody rites. It is no valid argument that in both religions, cruelty afterward became more or less an element. Whether Mr. Fergusson's hypothesis is well founded must be decided by other evidence.

CHAPTER VII.

VISITS TO PROMINENT PERSONS.

I WAS enabled, through the courtesy of Señor Don Matias Romero, the Mexican Minister at Washington, who furnished me with the necessary letter of introduction, to obtain an interview with the President of Mexico, General Manuel Gonzalez. He has seen much active service and was the commander who won the Battle of Tepeac, in the last revolution, which placed General Diaz in the Presidential chair, and which of course assured to him the succession; the Mexican Constitution prohibiting the immediate re-election of the President. At the present moment he suffers severely from the effects of wounds received in battle. I therefore found it necessary to call several times before he was able to receive me. He is a genial, pleasant gentleman of about fifty years of age, of middle height and is quite thick-set.

He has a very noticeable scar on his left cheek. It is said that he has received in all twenty-seven wounds, one of which caused the loss of his right arm.

Although he has travelled more or less in the United States he speaks no English, but he welcomed me with the utmost politeness in the Spanish language, declaring himself in glowing terms to be at my service and very happy to do anything that might add to my pleasure or convenience during my sojourn in Mexico.

He was very glad, he said, that the Americans were willing to invest their capital in building railroads in Mexico. He regarded their construction as a great benefit to his country. He felt assured that the trade which would result from it, provided it was supplemented by a commercial treaty, would be of great advantage not only to Mexico, but to the United States as well. It would also, he added, promote the friendly relations which happily now exist and which he hoped would forever continue between the two countries.

General Strother, the American Consul-General, remarking upon this subject, declared that it was chiefly owing to the action of the United States in sending General Phil Sheridan to the frontier with an army of observation, consisting of seventy thousand veterans, in the time of Maximilian, that any friendly feeling now exists on the part of the Mexicans towards our Government and people. Immediately after the war between the two countries, he added, a law had been passed, which is still in force, inhibiting aliens from acquiring title to land within twenty leagues of the boundary lines. The purpose of this legislation was to guard against possible encroachments on the part of the Americans.

I have ventured to refer to these remarks in order that I may record my dissent from the conclusion thus expressed. Throughout my entire sojourn in the Mexican Republic I made it my constant aim to inform myself regarding the sentiments of the people, high and low, rich and poor, towards us. It affords me no ordinary satisfaction to testify that, not only no bitter and resentful memories of the war now rankle in the breasts of our neighbors, but that a cordial feeling of friendship and community of interest is almost universally prevalent. All Mexicans thoroughly understand that the war was brought about by the ruffianly propagandists of slavery, for the purpose of strengthening the slave power and of rendering it supreme in the administration of our Government. Nothing could possibly have been more hateful in the eyes of our neighbors. Inspired by the teachings of the Church, they had, in advance of every other nation, eliminated from their laws and constitution the curse and scourge, the sin and shame, of negro slavery. When therefore a vast territory was wrested from them at the cost of many lives and an immense amount of treasure, and given over to slavery, it was not in human nature to look upon the result with composure. The War of the Rebellion having put an end to slavery in this country, the bands of peace and good-will towards each other have grown stronger and stronger with the lapse of time.

Among the letters of introduction furnished me by Señor Romero was one addressed to

Señor Don Ignacio Mariscal, the Minister of Foreign Relations. The functions of this officer correspond substantially to those of the Secretary of State under our own Government. I called on him at his office in the Government Palace, and was conducted through a series of elegantly furnished apartments to the parlor in which he received me. He is a very courteous and high-bred gentleman, and has perfect command of the English language, having lived some time in the United States. I advise all Americans visiting Mexico to seek an introduction to him.

Speaking of the relations of Mexico to the United States, he said that the Mexicans would like to have free trade between the two countries; but that his country was rather poor at present and required the revenues derived from duties on imports for its support, adding that a certain percentage of these duties had been irrevocably pledged to pay the subventions granted to the railroad companies. He thought that the United States Government might very well remove all duties from Mexican produce, because, as he understood the matter, the sole opposition to the proposed commercial treaty came from those who are engaged in the production of sugar and tobacco. The opposition of these interests, he thought, was not altogether just, as nearly all the sugar and tobacco raised in Mexico was required for home consumption —the quantity exported to the United States having thus far been very inconsiderable. Therefore Mexico could not bring these articles into serious competition with us until the resources of the country were more fully developed by the completion of the railways. He saw only one objection to the measure,—which was one that could be removed by judicious legislation on the part of both Governments. This objection was that sugar produced in Cuba and in the other West India Islands might be smuggled into the United States by way of Mexico. He knew, however, that this contraband trade is now carried on to an infinitely greater extent at our Pacific ports, where sugar from Peru is imported free of duty, under cover of the treaty of the United States with the Hawaiian Islands.

He spoke of the facilities for travelling about

the country, and remarked that he considered that the days of stage-coach robberies were passed and gone, owing to the new era in the history of the country and to the effective measures which the Government has taken to suppress the practice. He remarked that there had been no robberies on the routes leading to the United States for the last three years.

During my stay in the capital I had the pleasure of conferring with Señor Mariscal on several occasions. The information and advice with which he kindly favored me proved to be of the greatest advantage while visiting all portions of the country.

Of course I availed myself of an early opportunity to call upon the American Minister, the Hon. Philip H. Morgan, of Louisiana. The American Legation occupies a fine building situated on the Paseo, which is one of the most fashionable and attractive quarters of the city. While waiting in the ante-room, I observed a number of portraits of the former Ministers, and I was naturally gratified to see my grandfather's picture among the number. I was soon shown into the Minister's private office. Judge Morgan is a gentleman of imposing personal appearance and elegant manners. As a jurist he had achieved a brilliant reputation before leaving home. Almost his entire life has been spent on the bench. Just before coming to Mexico he had occupied the position of Judge of the International Court in Egypt. The United States is fortunate in having as its representative a gentleman who is so able and learned, and at the same time so popular and highly esteemed. He remarked that the interest which our people had lately taken in Mexican affairs had caused a great increase in the business of his office.

On learning that I intended to record the result of my observations, he said that matters were progressing so rapidly that what was written now was likely to require revision before many months had elapsed.

Judge Morgan and his family enjoy great personal popularity, and their numerous entertainments are held in pleasant remembrance by all those who have had the good fortune to attend them.

I am sure I shall render my countrymen who may hereafter have occasion to visit Mexico, an acceptable and valuable service by advising them to lose no time in seeking an interview with the Consul-General of the United States, the Hon. David H. Strother, of Virginia. The offices of the Consulate are situated in a building in the *Calle de la Perpetua*, which was once occupied by the Inquisition. A stone in the court-yard bears an inscription with the date 1598. General Strother is thoroughly informed on all matters relating to Mexico, and is a writer of acknowledged ability, having for years been a contributor to *Harper's Monthly Magazine*.

Extensive travel in many parts of the world has qualified him in an eminent degree to judge with accuracy not only the present condition but likewise the future prospects of Mexico, which he regards as exceedingly brilliant. He dwelt with great eloquence upon its boundless and inexhaustible natural resources; and he looks forward with confidence to their early development. He predicts that the present primitive methods employed in nearly every branch of industry will soon give place to improved processes; and that, by means of new facilities of transportation and domestic intercommunication, Mexico is destined to take a prominent place in the family of nations.

CHAPTER VIII.

A TRIP WESTWARD.

The desire to see one of the greatest of the natural wonders of the world now impelled me to make a trip to the volcano of Jorullo. It is situated almost due west from the capital, in the State of Michoacan, and less than one hundred miles from the Pacific Ocean. As it is a four days' journey from the nearest station on the Mexican National Railway, the excursion from the capital cannot be conveniently made in much less time than two weeks.

Accordingly, one afternoon, in the early part of the month of March last, I took the train at the temporary station near the new park; my brother, who had accompanied me to Mexico, being my companion. After crossing the valley the train ascended the mountain-wall, within which the city lies, by a series of heavy grades. I was soon enabled to see the valley of Mexico stretched out below me like a map. A gentleman sitting near me in the car called my attention to the grand spectacle, and with the animation characteristic of his race, he cried: "*Muy bonito! muy bonito! muy bonito!*" ("Very beautiful! very beautiful! very beautiful!")

At the end of two hours the train reached the highest point on the road, which is nine thousand nine hundred and seventy-four feet above the sea-level. I soon arrived at the city of Toluca, where I passed the night. This place is situated at the foot of the magnificent volcanic mountain of Toluca, the height of which is fifteen thousand one hundred and sixty-six feet above the sea-level. Consequently it is capped with eternal snow. The city itself has an elevation of eight thousand six hundred feet. It is a thriving place, and exhibits a degree of neatness seldom seen in Mexican cities. An admirable statue, in marble, of the Liberator Hidaigo, stands in the centre of the Plaza.

The hotel is unusually good. I was conducted to a clean and spacious apartment, newly painted; and I even ventured to sit down on the chairs without first testing their strength. Here, as in many other places, the dining-room is not under the same management as the hotel. A theatre, in a dilapidated condition, occupies the rear portion of the building.

A national industrial exposition has recently been held at Toluca. The enterprise was attended with great success. Immense numbers of people went daily from the capital to Toluca, returning in the afternoon. Numerous excursion trains were engaged, from day to day, by large parties which were formed for the purpose.

Expositions of this description seem to be very popular with the Mexicans, and have been lately held at the cities of Orizaba and Queretaro. Evidently they belong to the number of those events which cast their shadows before. Lithographic pictures representing the buildings used for these purposes were printed and circulated in large numbers throughout the Republic.

The next day's journey was through a high and desolate region chiefly devoted to grazing.

About noon the train stopped by the side of a stationary car in which a very good dinner was served. While I was sitting at the table a terrific hail-storm burst forth. From the noise of the hail-stones striking against the car it seemed as if the roof would be beaten in. On this, as well as on many previous occasions, I was much astonished at the apparent insensibility of the natives to the elements. Some of them seemed to give no heed whatever to the tempest, while others only protected themselves by putting on a mantle made of the fibres of the maguey plant, which, however, did not extend quite to the knees. Below that point their legs were entirely exposed, only a few even wearing sandals, although snow lay on the ground, the remains of a recent storm which had fallen in this elevated region. They also seemed to be perfectly indifferent whether or not they took refuge under some friendly cover.

At nightfall I had reached Maravatio, lying one hundred and twenty-nine miles west of the capital. At that time it was the temporary terminus of the road, but I have learned that the road has since been opened to the town of Acambaro. Repairing to the Hotel de Diligencias, from which the diligence for Morelia was advertised to leave at three o'clock on the following morning, I secured seats for myself and my brother. The hotel is a one-story building with a square court-yard in the centre from which the rooms open. The apartments which do not front on the street have no windows, and with their massive doors, with ponderous locks and keys, are suggestive of dungeons. On retiring, I debated the question whether I should turn the formidable key. Should the lock get out of order, or should anything occur, for instance a fire, to prevent the doors from being opened, the unfortunate prisoner would have no means of escape.

At supper the people around the hotel, consisting chiefly of American civil engineers in the employ of the Railway Company, with the train and station hands, beguiled the time with tales of the various stage-coach robberies which had recently occurred, as they said, in the vicinity. Perhaps their intentions were a trifle mischievous.

Promptly at three in the morning I was prepared to set out, but there were no signs of making ready the old and seemingly worn-out diligence, built in imitation of a Concord coach, which stood in the court-yard. At half after four the attendants began to grease the wheels and to make sundry repairs by the light of a small bonfire. After the lapse of another hour the eight mules were hitched up. First came two leaders, then four abreast and then two at the pole; and by six o'clock, three hours after the designated time of departure, I was on my way.

The storm of the preceding day had greatly injured the roads. Never very good, they were now in a shocking condition. With the rate of speed at which I was moving I concluded that, instead of making the distance to Morelia in one day, as advertised, the journey was likely to take at least twice that length of time. In the diligence, like a Mount Desert buck-board, the middle seats are the best, because your neighbors hold you in and make something soft to be occasionally pitched against.

If possible, the traveller should sit between two stout passengers. The drivers of diligences are provided with an assistant, whose duty it is to execute the orders of the driver, —above all to beat the mules. He uses a whip with a lash long enough to reach the leaders. He has also another with a short but unusually heavy lash, and when necessary, especially when the diligence is going up hill, he jumps down and applies it with effect. He also takes a supply of stones on the box, and when occasion requires he throws them at the leaders with unerring aim. The driver is also armed with a whip having a long lash. With all these powers of persuasion in operation, the perceptive faculties of an intelligent mule are apt to be sufficiently aroused to enable him to perceive that he is expected to move. Presently a stop was made to change mules, and the passengers went into a peon's house for breakfast. A peon is an Indian day-laborer.

The bill of fare consisted of chickens, eggs, boiled beans and *tortillas*. This cabin, which was better than the average, was absolutely devoid of anything that could justly be denominated luxuries. There were no beds, and no chairs. A large part of the Indian population never slept in a bed. These people sit on the ground, often gazing vacantly before them for hours. For the accommodation of the passengers some old boxes were brought out to serve for chairs. To my surprise, the table was furnished with a limited number of china plates, but there were no knives, forks or spoons. When eating food which cannot well be taken in the fingers, a *tortilla* is used as a kind of scoop to convey the food to the mouth. To the Mexican the *tortilla* is what the potato is to the peasant of the Emerald Isle. It is a flat cake, circular in form, about the size of an ordinary dinner-plate, and is made of Indian corn, moistened with water and thoroughly kneaded. The corn is placed on a flat stone. The *tortilla*-maker rests on her knees and holds a cylindrical stone with one hand on each end of it. She runs this stone back and forth on the flat stone on which she has placed the corn, and so crushes it by the pressure. Then by mixing water with the crushed corn she makes a kind of dough and continues to work this as before. Next she takes a quantity of dough between her hands and by patting it for a time gives it the proper shape and size. She then bakes it on a large earthen plate resting over a small fire. When away from home or on a journey the peons take a supply of *tortillas* with them, and they appear to desire no other food. I have seen them at night in the open fields gathered around fires over which they were toasting their *tortillas*, which are not considered good unless they are freshly baked or warmed up. In places distant from the centres of population bread is seldom to be found and *tortillas* are served in its place.

How long the *tortilla* has been in use it is impossible to say. Historians record that when the Spaniards entered the country, in the beginning of the sixteenth century, they found it to be the national article of diet. The soldiers, unable to procure any more acceptable food, were obliged to accustom themselves to its use, as indeed travellers frequently are even in our day. In future ages, antiquarians will doubtless speculate upon the question as to what race of people first invented the *tortilla*, whether the Aztec, the Toltec, or the still more remote Olmec.

In physique, the peons are far inferior to the laboring men in the United States, but their deficiency of muscular power is somewhat counterbalanced by their power of endurance and ability to bear exposure to the elements. In one instance, while on a horse-back tour, a well-formed, erect and athletic-looking Indian of about fifty-five years of age was able to keep up with my horse for nearly thirty-two miles. To the last he walked gracefully, with head erect and chest well expanded. He wore the usual dress of coarse cotton cloth, with his trousers rolled up as far as possible, and sandals on his feet. He followed me across plain and over mountain. When I put my horse into a faster pace he would break into a run, never seeming to tire. All this time I held no conversation with him, because, although perfectly good-natured, he seemed to be of a taciturn disposition.

The pay per day of an ordinary agricultural laborer is one real and a half, or eighteen and three-quarter cents. Those employed on large *haciendas* are paid off in part by store-orders, which of course greatly reduces the cost to the employer, and correspondingly swindles the luckless laborer out of his just due. Then the produce of the land is sold to him at a very exorbitant price, so that the peon's nominal pay of eighteen and three-quarter cents per day does not in reality amount to much more than half that sum. Meek in his disposition, with few wants, he submits to this and indeed to any other species of imposition without complaint. While at work he keeps it in his mind that there are holidays in store for him in the future, and of these, the holiday season of Holy Week is observed and enjoyed with the greatest possible delight. Then he spends the little money he has hoarded for his enjoyment and that of his family. If possible, he will take them with him to the capital, or at least to the nearest town of importance. At these seasons of festivity an enormous quantity of *pulque* is consumed, and drunken men and women reel through the streets of the cities. Only when their money has vanished will they return to their homes. There they enter with apparent cheerfulness upon another long period of unremitting toil and privation in order to accumulate means for the so-called enjoyment of other holidays to come.

Setting out once more I passed through the town of Acambaro, where five mounted soldiers belonging to the Rural Guards made their appearance. They accompanied the diligence for the remainder of the day to a small town called Zinapecuaro. Here the passengers spent the night at the little diligence tavern. Everything was old and dilapidated, but the landlord and his people were very obliging and made their guests as comfortable as circumstances would permit. It is evident that foreigners seldom make their way into this part of the Republic. I now became an object of curiosity and even amusement. At first everybody with whom I conversed seemed to presume that I was travelling on business connected with the railways. When they learned their mistake they showed great surprise. It was evidently unprecedented for *viajeros particulares*, or tourists, to invade their territory.

The passengers were ready to start promptly at six o'clock the next morning, and after rattling for a time over the cobble-stone pavements of the town, the diligence entered upon a long stretch of good road, and the mules galloped along briskly in the cool atmosphere of the early dawn. The rising sun disclosed the beauties of a fertile and well-cultivated plain resembling the valley of the Connecticut River.

The rain of the preceding day had lent an unusual freshness to the vegetation, the weather was perfect, the surroundings most picturesque. Everything seemed to be so pleasant and attractive that I shall always remember this early morning drive as one of the most pleasing incidents of my travels. Soon came a more hilly region, and on the left, lying among a range of picturesque mountains, Lake Cuitzeo, the second lake in size in Mexico, was visible.

The Rural Guards rode with the diligence from each town in succession until the next was reached, when they were relieved by those belonging to that station, the first squad returning home. They were in the practice, however, of turning back about a mile too soon, and if brigands had desired to attack us they would have had an ample opportunity to make the attempt during these intervals. These robbers often meet with a warm reception from the passengers themselves, as everybody in Mexico goes armed, and, except, perhaps, when in the larger cities, their weapons are worn in plain sight. During the last few years there has been much less brigandage in the country than formerly. This is due in a great measure to the fact that the Government has done everything in its power to suppress the practice. The soldiers hunted down a large number of the highwaymen, and those who were too wary or too powerful to be entrapped have been bought off by receiving commissions in the army. Once enlisted they renounce all their former associations and even pursue their former confederates with relentless zeal. Knowing just who the brigands are, and where to find them, of course these men become the most effective agents for the Government.

Another reason, perhaps, for the less frequent occurrence of stage-coach robberies, is the opportunity to earn an honest living which has of late been afforded by the construction of the various railway lines. It need hardly be remarked that this decreases the number of the destitute and removes in a great degree the temptation to commit crime. With the exception of the States of Jalisco and Sinaloa, where intestine troubles exist which have long defied the efforts of the Government for their suppression, there are now fewer organized bands of robbers in the country than ever before. A Roman Catholic priest from Guadalajara, the capital of the State of Jalisco, and only second in size to the City of Mexico, having a population of eighty-eight thousand, told me that highway robberies are of almost daily occurrence in his State, and that the highwaymen take not only the valuables of the victims but even require them to give up the clothes which they are wearing.

Desperate men abound in almost every part

of the country who are ready to seize any opportunity to obtain possession by a bold stroke of a considerable amount of money or valuables. For this, among other reasons, everybody carries a revolver in full view. The natural aversion to dying young, it is thought, may prevent an attempt at robbery which might be made upon an unarmed man.

Standing in front of one of the post-stations while the mules were changed, I had an opportunity to see a specimen of the horsemanship for which the Mexicans are so famous. A peon was mounted on a vicious horse. The animal tried his best to unseat his rider, going through all the various motions of rearing, plunging, bucking and kicking, yet the man sat with perfect composure as firmly in his saddle as if he had been a part of the horse. At times it seemed as though the girths of the saddle would not stand the strain; but the horse at last perceiving that his efforts to free himself were of no avail, became as quiet as a lamb.

From the commencement of this trip I had had as a fellow-passenger in the diligence a very polite elderly gentleman. He was known to almost everybody on the road, and everywhere was treated with extraordinary deference. The landlord of the hotel where the passengers had passed the night, provided a bed for him in his private parlor. I afterwards learned that he was a prominent commission merchant of the City of Morelia. He politely presented me with his card, which bore the name "Manuel Lozano." When the diligence stopped for breakfast, he paid the entire bill. I offered to pay my share, explaining that such was the custom in my own country, but he declined to listen to my proposition. In the course of my journeyings I subsequently observed that it is the frequent practice, especially in provincial districts, for some one passenger in the diligence to pay the bill, for breakfast or dinner, of the entire company, although they all happened to be total strangers.

Señor Lozano extended to me many other courtesies, which on several occasions were very marked. Meeting him one day in the street, in Morelia, he greeted me with the greatest cordiality. Pointing to his residence, which was about a block distant, with the most courtly politeness he said to me, in Spanish: "The third house with a lamp in front of it,—that is your house."

At a place some miles distant from the end of the journey a gentleman entered the diligence to whom he at once introduced me. This was Señor Don Pedro Rangel, one of the thirteen members of the Legislature of the State of Michoacan, and a brother-in-law of the Governor of that State. Señor Rangel related many interesting and instructive facts concerning the history and politics of Michoacan. At our parting he promised to call upon me at my hotel and introduce me to the Governor, Señor Don Pudenciano Dorantes.

Nine hours' journeying from the place of starting in the morning brought me to the City of Morelia, the capital of the State of Michoacan. With a grand flourish the diligence drove up a long paved avenue, well shaded with trees, and stopped at the diligence hotel. I alighted and walked to the Hotel de la Soledad, the most distinguished public house of the city.

True to his promise, Señor Rangel paid me a visit in the evening, and accompanied me to the Governor's residence. His Excellency is an accomplished gentleman, cordial in his manners and of remarkably prepossessing appearance. I was also honored with an introduction to Señora Dorantes, who had entered the room when I was presented to her husband.

The Governor spoke of the projected railways, and expressed the hope that they might be completed through the State of Michoacan at an early day. He was very certain that the productions of that region, which consist principally of coffee and tropical fruits, with the facilities of transportation thus afforded would find a remunerative market in the United States.

I learned afterwards that this expectation is generally entertained in this region. The prominent inhabitants speak enthusiastically of the completion of railway connection with the United States, and the consequent introduction of American capital and enterprise as certain to inaugurate a new and better state of things in Mexico. Many of them at present are "land-poor." They own mines of great richness, but they have not the means for working them. Some of these mine-owners keep retail stores in the arcades. It is the universal belief that, when the railways are in full operation, there will be a great influx of Americans. They confidently hope to enlist our countrymen in their various enterprises, and by this means to emancipate themselves from their chronic condition of embarrassment, both personal and national.

My host at the hotel participated in the general anticipation. He and his wife were diligently studying English, so as to be prepared for the Americans when they should come. He was constantly greeting me with such expressions as these: "Be pleased to be seated, sir;" "I am your humble servant, sir." I am apprehensive when the Americans become numerous in Morelia, and large returns are made from mining and agriculture, that the hotel accommodations will become more costly. I found good hotels there, but the prices were very moderate. I took my meals at the best restaurant in the city at an expense of about one dollar and a quarter per day, which is less than one-half of the cost in the capital.

The State of Michoacan, formerly known as the Intendancy of Valladolid, is still largely inhabited by a native population. It abounds with valuable mines; the principal of which, that of Tlalpujahua, is situated close to the mountains of Campo del Gallo, where the illustrious patriot Hidalgo established a foundry for the casting of cannon. The City of Morelia, its capital, is well built and is kept very clean. The remarkable air of quietude which reigns here is very pleasing to a tired and wayworn traveller. It is suggestive, however, of the solution that the business and commercial enterprises of the city are not at present very active.

The ecclesiastical buildings are of a high order. The Cathedral is a magnificent structure, built in the Spanish Renaissance style. That eminent architect, James Renwick, Esq., to whom I have exhibited photographic views of it, pronounces it to be the most perfect and admirable specimen of that order of architecture which has fallen under his observation.

While the church edifices in other States of the Mexican Republic are many of them neglected and going rapidly into decay, those of the State of Michoacan are kept in excellent repair. Indeed, in one place I observed workmen engaged in erecting a new stone tower on one of the oldest churches. Priests throng the streets in their long black gowns and stove-pipe hats, and the bells seem to ring incessantly. Michoacan is one of the strongholds of the Roman Catholic Church, and all the numerous outward forms of the Roman ritual are observed in the strictest manner. Its partisans are very exacting in matters of devotion. I was actually insulted in the City of Morelia for having neglected to remove my hat when passing the Cathedral, although it was at night and I was on the opposite side of the wide street upon which that fine edifice stands.

Governor Dorantes very graciously extended to me numerous civilities. On my departure he furnished me with official letters to the *Pre-*

fectos of the towns of Patzcuaro and Ario, through which I would pass on my way to the volcano of Jorullo. These missives directed those magistrates to render me every service and extend to me every civility in their power.

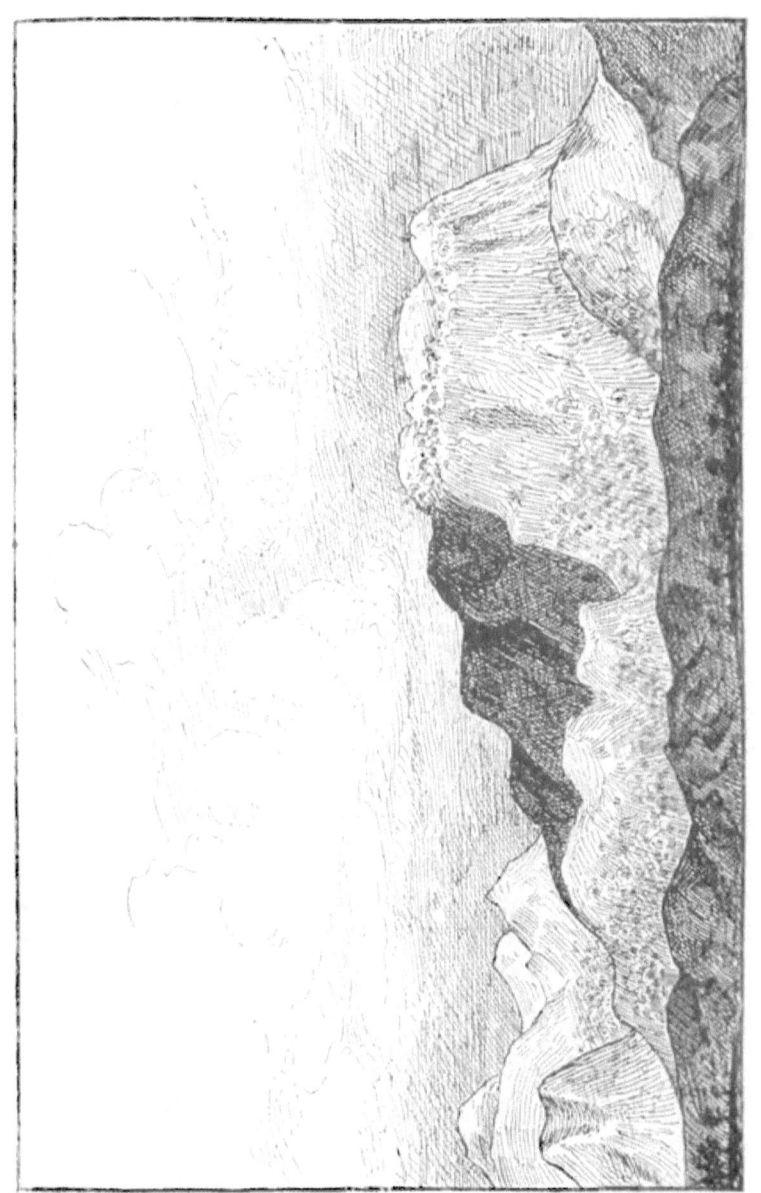

VOLCANO OF JORULLO.
From a pen and ink sketch by the Author.

CHAPTER IX.

THE VOLCANO OF JORULLO.

THE General Diligence Company, which controls nearly all the stage-coach lines in the Republic, runs no vehicles westward of Morelia. Finding, however, that I could reach Patzcuaro by a *"diligencia particular,"* I took passage, at half after five o'clock on the following morning, for that town, which is sixteen leagues distant. Distances are reckoned in Mexico by the Spanish league, which is equal to two and twelve-nineteenths English miles. The road at first is rocky and often nearly impassable. When appealed to by the driver, who was at the same time the proprietor of the vehicle, the passengers would good-naturedly alight and walk a short distance. After a while the road somewhat improved. While passing through a mountain range, the scenery became picturesque. The beautiful City of Morelia continued in sight for several hours.

The draught animals were changed twice on the trip. At the second change, I was surprised to find instead of the mule-teams which had brought me thus far, a relay of eight spirited horses led out from the stable. The reason for this presently appeared. Rival lines send out diligences three times a week on the same day and at the same hour. Up to this point they had proceeded at a moderate pace as if by mutual consent. Now a struggle for the lead was about to begin. The passengers had not quite finished their breakfast, when the drivers began to call out : " *Vamonos ! Vamonos !* " ("Let us go! Let us go!") Everybody was at once on the *qui vive*. Our horses reared and plunged ; and when loosed from the grasp of the hostlers, dashed straight at the fence of the yard, but the driver with great dexterity guided them through a narrow gateway. A stage-coach race, with eight horses at their utmost speed, is apt to prove interesting to the passengers inside. In this instance it hastened them rapidly to their journey's end. Our driver, a handsome and portly man of distinguished appearance, was a " stunning " fellow, as Thackeray would say. Resplendent in a hat richly ornamented with silver, a short jacket made of purple plush, a colored shirt, a red sash and long leather leggings, he was altogether the *beau ideal* of a stage driver. Like men of his craft in other parts of the world, he was evidently a sort of autocrat on the road, to whom people paid court, and whose smile produced joy in the hearts of those who were fortunate enough to be favored by it. One evening I invited him to dine with me, and found him to be an exceedingly polite man, well versed in the conventionalities of the dinner table.

At the outset we had a trifle the better of the contest; but the opposition coach had a lighter load and presently began to make faster headway. Our driver, however, was equal to the exigency, and pulled his horses into the road in front of those of his adversary. But this headlong pace could not last to the end; the strain was too great. Besides, one of our horses somehow entangled his forelegs in the harness, compelling us to stop in order to extricate him. This was the rival driver's opportunity. He dashed by at full speed, and we were unable to overtake him until we had reached the City of Patzcuaro. There I found an excellent hotel, with good accommodations; while the prices in the restaurant seemed to me ridiculously low: an excellent dinner was served for thirty cents.

The principal object of interest here is the lake of Patzcuaro, about five leagues long from north-east to south-west, and twelve leagues in circumference. It is bordered by mountains, which are covered with trees, and presents a beautiful and picturesque appearance, reminding one of a great mirror set in a frame of arabesque. It also contains five small islands, which are covered with a luxuriant vegetation, interspersed with brilliant flowers. I can recall no landscape which surpasses it in loveliness.

Several miles to the eastward of the lake is an extinct volcano, within the crater of which is now a flourishing field of wheat.

There being no public conveyance of any kind beyond this place, I engaged the services of a *mozo*, or servant, whose duties are the same as those of a courier in continental Europe. He procured the necessary saddle-horses, and I set out early the following morning for the town of Ario, a distance of twelve leagues. The road lay through the mountains, as before. I met with numerous trains of pack-mules and donkeys, laden with the produce of the region —fruits, coffee, cotton, palm-leaves and copper ore. The latter was from the old mines of San Pedro de Jorullo, which were worked by the Aztecs long before the coming of the Spaniards. On their return trip, these trains carry imported articles. These goods by the time they reach the towns near the Pacific coast, become enhanced in cost to an extent which is bewildering to a stranger.

Ario is a squalid hamlet, and the hotel is, if possible, still more miserable; probably few Americans have set foot within its limits in our day. I was stared at by everybody. The children congregated around the door of the restaurant and watched me while at dinner, which cost but eighteen cents. Almost every idler in the town was present to superintend the cleaning of my shoes.

I paid my respects to the *Prefecto*, and delivered to him Governor Dorantes' letter. He received me with distinguished civility, and loaned me his fine saddle-horse for an afternoon ride. With a somewhat extensive observation and experience of saddle-horses in various parts of this country, as well as in the British islands and on the continent of Europe, I have no hesitation in saying that many of the Mexican horses are fully equal to the best which I have met with elsewhere. In general they are rather small, resembling in that particular the Arabian horses. Probably few, if any of them, are thoroughbred. Still, I am of the opinion that a large number have a strain of Arabian blood. Their extraordinary endurance denotes this.

The *Prefecto* likewise gave me a letter of credence to an official who lived at the foot of the volcano; and when I set out the ensuing morning, he sent a mounted escort under the command of a corporal with me, not, as he said, because it was necessary for my protection, but as a mark of respect to the authority of the Governor, whose guest I was. They accompanied me for many miles, observing to the very last the strictest military etiquette. I soon found myself in the midst of scenery of the greatest grandeur. The Cordilleras towered aloft on every side. The volcano of Jorullo belongs to this system. Continuing my journey by abrupt descents, I soon reached a plain having an elevation of about two thousand feet, yet belonging to the *Tierras Calientes* of the Pacific slope. Having come eight leagues, I stopped for refreshment at a hamlet called Tejamanil. The houses, with the exception of an old *hacienda* building, were constructed of rough planks fastened together with ropes or some other expedient equally simple and primitive, and thatched with palm-leaves. This style of architecture is older than the Spanish Conquest. The mode of living was still more antique. Human beings, horses, mules, donkeys, dogs, pigs and chickens dwelt together, all in perfect harmony and dirt. Although it was the ninth day of

March, which is not the hot season, the mercury stood in the shade at eighty-nine degrees, Fahrenheit.

I waited here till the heat had somewhat moderated, and then went on to La Puerta de la Playa, which is situated near the base of the volcano. I presented my letter from the *Prefecto* of Ario to the official, Señor Don Francisco Vega, who immediately invited me to make his house my home during my stay. I was glad to accept his invitation. The next morning I arose at four o'clock, in order to avoid the heat while making the ascent. To my surprise, my host, although a man advanced in years, had also risen, and with exquisite courtesy communicated his purpose to accompany me. Mounting our horses, we rode on in the dark as far as this was practicable, and then left the animals in the care of the *mozo*.

The mountain rises very abruptly from the plain, to a height of about two thousand feet. The ascent does not require any especial skill in the matter of climbing, but the walking is very laborious. The path lies over soft ashes, which are continually sliding from under the feet, and over loose, irregular masses of lava. At sunrise I stood on the summit, and looked down a descent of six hundred feet into a crater about eighteen hundred feet long and of nearly the same breadth. In numerous places steam was issuing in small quantities from fissures. The volcano is less than a mile wide at any point on the summit, but it is much larger than that at the base. A mass of lava was emitted at the last eruption almost as large as the body of the mountain itself.

A hundred and twenty-five years ago the place was a palmy plain, occupied as a *hacienda*. One hot September evening, in the year 1759, the surface of the ground began gradually to rise, while a strange sound was heard beneath the earth. Flames issued forth, fragments of rock were hurled upward, and the eruption continued for many months. This was the beginning of Mount Jorullo. Baron von Humboldt describes the occurrence as one of the most extraordinary revolutions in the history of our planet. "Till the middle of the eighteenth century," says he, "fields cultivated with sugar-cane and indigo occupied the extent of ground between the two brooks called Cuitamba and San Pedro. They were bounded by basaltic mountains, of which the structure seems to indicate that all this country at a very remote period had been already several times convulsed by volcanoes. These fields, watered by artificial means, belonged to the plantation (*hacienda*) of San Pedro de Jorullo, one of the greatest and richest of the country. In the month of June, 1759, a subterraneous noise was heard. Hollow noises of a most alarming nature (*bramidos*) were accompanied by frequent earthquakes, which succeeded one another for from fifty to sixty days, to the great consternation of the inhabitants of the *hacienda*.

"From the beginning of September, everything seemed to announce the complete re-establishment of tranquillity, when in the night between the twenty-eighth and twenty-ninth, the horrible subterraneous noise recommenced. The affrighted Indians fled to the mountains of Aquasarco. A tract of ground from three to four square miles in extent, which goes by the name of *Malpays,* rose up in the shape of a bladder. The bounds of this convulsion are still distinguishable in the fractured strata. The *Malpays* near its edges is only twelve metres above the old level of the plain called the *playas de Jorullo;* but the convexity of the ground thus thrown up increases progressively toward the centre to an elevation of one hundred and sixty metres.

"Those who witnessed this great catastrophe from the top of Aquasarco assert that flames were seen to issue forth for the extent of more than half a square mile ; that fragments of burning rocks were thrown up to prodigious heights; and that through a thick cloud of ashes, illumined by the volcanic fire, the softened surface of the earth was seen to swell up like an agitated sea. The rivers of Cuitamba and San Pedro precipitated themselves into the burning chasms. The decomposition of the water contributed to invigorate the flames, which were distinguishable at the City of Patzcuaro, though situated on a very extensive table-land fourteen hundred metres elevated above the plains of *las playas de Jorullo*. Eruptions of mud, and especially strata of clay, enveloping balls of decomposing basalts in concentric layers, appear to indicate that subterraneous water had no small share in producing this extraordinary revolution. Thousands of small cones, called by the indigenes *ovens* (*hornitos*), issued forth from the *Malpays*. Although within the last fifteen years,* according to the testimony of the Indians, the heat of these volcanic ovens has suffered a great diminution, I have seen the thermometer rise to ninety-five [203° F.] on being plunged into fissures which exhale an aqueous vapor. Each small cone is a *fumarola*, from which a thick vapor ascends to the height of ten or fifteen metres. In many of them a subterraneous noise is heard, which appears to announce the proximity of a fluid in ebullition.

"In the midst of the ovens six large masses

---

* Baron von Humboldt and M. Bonpland made the ascent of Mount Jorullo on the nineteenth of September, 1803. He accordingly refers to it at a period of more than forty years after the first eruption.

elevated from four to five hundred metres each above the old level of the plains sprung up from a chasm, of which the direction is from the N.N.E. to the S.S.E. This is the phenomenon of the Monte Novo of Naples, several times repeated in a range of volcanic hills. The most elevated of these enormous masses, which bears some resemblance to the *puys* de l'Auvergne, is the great Volcan de Jorullo. It is continually burning, and has thrown up from the north side an immense quantity of scorified and basaltic lavas containing fragments of primitive rocks. These great eruptions of the central volcano continued till the month of February, 1760. In the following years they became gradually less frequent. The Indians, frightened at the horrible noises of the new volcano, abandoned at first all the villages situated within seven or eight leagues' distance of the *playas de Jorullo*. They became gradually, however, accustomed to this terrific spectacle; and having returned to their cottages they advanced towards the mountains of Aquasarco and Santa Inez, to admire the streams of fire discharged from an infinity of great and small volcanic apertures. The roofs of the houses of Queretaro were then covered with ashes at a distance of more than forty-eight leagues in a straight line from the scene of the explosion. Although the subterraneous fire now appears far from violent and the *Malpays* and the great volcano begin to be covered with vegetation, we nevertheless found the ambient air heated to such a degree by the activity of the small ovens (*hornitos*), that the thermometer, at a great distance from the surface, and in the shade, rose as high as forty-three degrees [109° F.]. This fact appears to prove that there is no exaggeration in the accounts of several old Indians who affirm that, for many years after the first eruption, the plains of Jorullo, even at a great distance from the scene of the explosion, were uninhabitable, from the excessive heat which prevailed in them."

The Baron gives other interesting details in regard to this volcano and the adjacent region. The two rivers of Cuitamba and San Pedro disappeared on the night of the explosion; but at a distance of a mile and a quarter farther west, two rivers burst forth from the ground, which the inhabitants declared to be the same streams, asserting that they heard great masses of water running underground in a westerly direction.

The view from the summit of Jorullo is magnificent. The mountain, to be sure, is by no means as high as many of those surrounding it; but the more lofty elevations are remote, and therefore interpose no serious obstruction. I saw the volcano of Colima, snow-capped and a hundred and twenty-five miles distant, with perfect distinctness. It is but ten miles from the Pacific Ocean, and is still active.

Before setting out to return it was resolved to descend into the crater. This was an undertaking attended with considerable personal risk. There is great danger of displacing the loose masses of lava and of thereby starting a landslide. We were fortunate enough, however, to make our way down in safety. Placing a thermometer into one of the fissures from which steam was issuing, the mercury registered one hundred and thirty-two degrees, Fahrenheit.

Easy as we had found the descent, we did not climb the wall of the crater with equal facility. It was not so difficult at first, but became more so as we approached nearer the edge. The others had succeeded in reaching a firm foothold on the summit, and I was not far behind them, when on a sudden the loose stones and pieces of lava on my left gave way and began to roll and slide downward. I had accidentally displaced several of the stones beneath, which however had served as a support to the others. I lost the hold of my left hand and foot, but fortunately my right hand was grasping a firm rock, in a crevice of which my right foot rested comparatively secure. I could only remain quiet in this position. Every attempt to advance, or even to place myself in a safer position, served only to increase the moving of the rubbish which hung trembling around me. My brother now hastened to my assistance. He stepped upon a rock which was firmly embedded, and taking fast hold of it with both hands, he reached his foot down for me to grasp. Holding on to it with one hand, I was able to make my way upward, and in a moment more was out of the treacherous crater. We now passed rapidly down the hill, running along the inclined planes of volcanic ashes. Reaching the horses in a short time, we mounted and returned to the house of our polite host. It being now mid-day we indulged in the *siesta* which the fierce heat of tropical latitudes renders so refreshing. As soon as the heat had in some degree subsided I set out on my return to Ario. The road ascends almost immediately over a thousand feet, when I rested for a time in the delightful shade of a noble pine grove.

By night I reached Ario. Not having been pleased with the hotel where I had sojourned the previous day, I now engaged rooms at another. But alas! there was little, if any, improvement in the surroundings. Whoever goes to either of these hostelries is certain to wish that he had gone to the other. The bedsteads consisted of planks, and had no mattresses or bed-clothing of any kind. The traveller is expected to content himself with the blanket which every Mexican carries with him.

The next day I set out for the capital, passing

through scenes similar to those experienced on my outward journey. At Morelia I was again treated with the utmost politeness, I had almost said distinction. Several gentlemen holding official positions paid their respects to me and showed me the most flattering attentions. They kindly chose to regard my visit to Mexico, and in particular my excursion to the volcano of Jorullo, which by no possibility could have any purpose of pecuniary profit, as being in some sense personally complimentary to themselves. A wealthy citizen, who had been a merchant, but who had retired from business, politely devoted almost an entire day to my entertainment. His house was one of the most elegant in the city. Much of his time was devoted to scientific pursuits. Conducting me to the roof of his house at night, he pointed out among the other constellations that of the magnificent Southern Cross, which, in this latitude, rises above the horizon.

CHAPTER X.

CUERNAVACA.

I ALSO paid a visit to the celebrated City of Cuernavaca, once the beloved residence of Cortez, and more recently the favorite retreat of the Emperor Maximilian. The diligence left the Hotel Iturbide, promptly at six o'clock in the morning. For several hours I was driven over a broad, smooth avenue, bordered on either side with trees, and extending through the suburbs of San Angel and those of Tlalpam. During all this time the route lay in close proximity to Lake Xochimilco. Presently I reached the foot of the mountain barrier which bounds the Valley of Mexico. Still the road was in excellent condition, far better, indeed, than any other I met with in the Republic. The ascent to the higher level is accordingly at once easy and delightful. A point was at length attained which is ten thousand feet above the level of the sea, and which overlooks the magnificent region just traversed. A little farther on I passed the divide, and the City of Cuernavaca lay before me in its wonderful beauty. It is situated on the side of the mountain, fully four thousand feet below the ground upon which I stood. At the left towered the spectral peaks of Popocatepetl and Iztaccihuatl. They continued in full view during the remainder of the drive. The road now descended. At the last place of changing, five mules were attached to the diligence, instead of eight, as is usual. I now made a high rate of speed, and reached the place of destination at four o'clock in the afternoon.

Cuernavaca is built on a projecting piece of land between two *barrancas*, or ravines, its altitude above the sea being between five thousand feet and six thousand feet. It was founded by the Nahuas five hundred years ago. They named it *Quauhnahuac*, The Town by the Beautiful Hills. In time it became tributary to the Aztecs, from whom it was wrested by Cortez in 1521. It afterwards became the personal property of the Conqueror, who took up his residence there in 1530. It had been the capital of the Tlahuico natives. Cortez built, at great cost, a splendid palace, as well as a church and convent for the Franciscans, believing that he was laying the foundations of a great metropolis. He also expended large sums upon the cultivation of the soil. He established large pastures for the rearing of fine cattle and merino sheep. But his fond anticipations of the coming glory of the lovely city, it need hardly be remarked, were never realized.

Until the year 1869, this district formed a part of the State of Mexico. It then became a separate State, receiving the title of Morelos, in honor of the distinguished priest of that name, elsewhere referred to, who had done such signal service as a general in the Mexican Revolution. Cuernavaca was again made its capital. It has a population of twelve thousand, and contains several churches, two of which belong to the Protestants, besides several other buildings of local importance. The inhabitants urge strangers to visit the *Recreo de Maximiliano*, a house about a mile and a half from town, where the unfortunate Emperor at times sought a respite from the cares and perplexities of state.

I may here remark that I have endeavored in vain to comprehend the impelling motive which prompts the Mexicans, of all conditions in life, to point out, importunately, every spot which is in any manner associated with the life and death of the man Maximilian. Evidently, the motive is not to heap obloquy upon his memory, or to exult in his miserable doom.

The palace of Cortez stands on the edge of one of the ravines, and commands a view of the part of the valley which was granted by the King of Spain to the *Conquistador.*

The picturesque gardens of La Borda, by reason of their singular beauty, are among the chief attractions of this enchanting spot. The landscape gardener who designed them was a master in his vocation, which, in such hands, is justly entitled to take its place with sculpture, painting and architecture, as one of the fine arts. None will deny that he exhibited an exquisite taste and skill. Let us hope that they may be preserved in their integrity, in order that, like the Boboli Gardens, like the gardens of the Villa Palavicini, and, like the Royal Gardens of Versailles, they may instruct and delight generations yet unborn.

From my window, which overlooked the plaza, I witnessed the funeral of one of the public men of the city. It was conducted in essentially the same manner as we are accustomed to conduct such an observance in the United States. Everybody seemed to have come out. Those who had high black hats put them on in order to do honor to the occasion. The heat was excessive, but every one seemed to be having a good time. The liquor-sellers, I may add, did a thriving business.

Sheltered as Cuernavaca is on all sides from the cold winds of the grand *plateau*, the climate is singularly mild and delightful. Its luxuriant vegetation is characteristic of the Torrid, rather than of the Temperate Zone. My visit was made in the middle of the month of March last. At dinner my landlady served for dessert an excellent watermelon. The charge for it was twenty-five cents. At the Iturbide restaurant, in the City of Mexico, it would have been two dollars. Although the distance between the two places is but fifty miles, the only means of transporting the watermelon to the capital is on the back of a mule or donkey; hence the difference in price.

CHAPTER XI.

COMMERCE.

IN our day it is common to use the term *Commerce* to denote a mercantile intercourse with foreign countries; while *Trade* is used to denote traffic between the inhabitants of the same country. Strictly speaking, there is no foundation for this distinction. Each is entitled, both by etymology and by decisive authority, to a comprehensive and general interpretation.

From the earliest ages, the development of civilization has always been characterized by the division of employments and by the exchange of the products of labor. Like the wild animal, the untutored savage has no trade. Like the brute, he instinctively wars upon the rights and property of his neighbor. As soon as he enters into social relations with others, and recognizes the justice of equivalents for the services and benefits which he receives, he ceases, to that extent, to be a savage. The interchange of good offices and the exchange of articles of value, regulated and facilitated by the adoption of compacts, denote a moral and intellectual advancement, which forms the condition precedent of all civilized society. Hence commerce may be regarded as being at once the means and the evidence of civility and enlightenment.

The welfare, prosperity and greatness of a people are undeniably dependent, in a very large measure, upon its commercial relations with other communities. So well is this now understood, that all civilized nations maintain, as far as practicable, peace and amity with each other, as the basis, and for the promotion, of commerce. A wise policy would seem to dictate that no impediments to its exercise should be interposed, by means of embargoes, taxes or restrictions of any other kind.

Agriculture brings out the wealth of the soil, supplying the human family with food and with many other articles of prime necessity. Mining extracts from the bowels of the earth the various mineral treasures. Skilled industry transforms the raw materials thus produced into textile fabrics and into various other instrumentalities for the use and enjoyment of mankind. It is the function of commerce to place these several commodities within the reach of every consumer, on such conditions as shall render them available for his wants. The trend of political economy, in recent times, has accordingly been in the direction of facilitating communication between districts and countries, in order to encourage the production and exchange of the merchandise and manufactures of each for the advantage of all.

These elementary truths have, of late, not only engaged, to a greater extent than ever before, the attention of the thinking men of Mexico, but it is evident that they are gradually gaining a footing on the popular mind. It is to be regretted that our sister Republic, like ourselves, and indeed like every other civilized nation, has its heritage of debt and prejudice to trammel the introduction of sound economical principles into its administrative policy.

The Mexican Constitution of 1857 favors to

the utmost possible extent a liberal policy; but the disturbed condition of affairs, incident chiefly to the French occupation, has retarded its fruition. That policy now bids fair to be realized. The Government is steadily, and it may even be said rapidly, removing all obstacles that impede the development of industry and, at the same time, discourage immigration.

However national obligations may interfere with the adoption of a liberal policy, as regards the foreign commerce of the country, I am not aware that the domestic commerce of Mexico differs essentially from that of the United States. In both countries, commerce between the several States is happily untrammelled. In both countries, the intercourse of the inhabitants with each other is of far greater importance, perhaps it is no exaggeration to say of a hundred-fold greater importance, than that with foreign nations. It is accordingly gratifying to know that this view of the subject receives the earnest attention of the enlightened statesmen who are now at the head of public affairs.

The primary need of the country is unquestionably commercial facilities, to the end that the products of the soil, as well as those of the mines, may be placed in the markets of the world without being burdened with a cost of transportation which practically is equivalent to prohibition. On the other hand, it is no less essential that the necessaries of civilized life should be introduced and delivered to the consumer on as favorable terms as they are brought into the adjacent countries.

A few facts may serve to illustrate more effectually than pages of dissertation the deficiency which is here referred to. On my way from the City of Cuernavaca to the capital, I met three *cargadores* (porters) on the highway, carrying a new set of furniture on their backs. The first of them had on his shoulders a sofa of considerable size, secured by straps across his forehead and breast, and passing under his arms; the second bore two large and heavy arm-chairs; the third carried several smaller chairs. They had evidently come from the City of Mexico, which was thirty-five miles distant. Firewood costing two dollars a cord at Patzcuaro, in the State of

Michoacan, sells in the capital for sixteen dollars a cord. At San Luis Potosi a shopkeeper showed me an invoice of snuff which was purchased in the city of New Orleans for the sum of nine dollars. Of course it was not manufactured in that city, so that the sum in question probably included not less·than three several profits, to wit: that of the manufacturer, that of the shipper, and, finally, that of the merchant. With the duty and the cost of transportation added, the package cost, at its destination, exactly fifty dollars. At Tejamanil, seven miles from the volcano of Jorullo, I purchased a merino scarf of French fabrication. At the *Bon Marché* in Paris, I could have bought it for fifteen, or, at the outside, twenty *sous*. At Tejamanil it cost a dollar.

The ports of the Republic open to foreign commerce are: Vera Cruz, Tampico, Matamoros, Campeachy, Progreso, Tabasco, Huatulco, Acapulco, Manzanillo, San Blas, Mazatlan, Altata, and Guaymas. The Mexican Railway extends from the first of these to the capital. It is contemplated to connect several others of these ports with the railroads now in progress or projected, and to establish regular lines of steamers touching at each in succession, which will run to the ports of this country and to those of Europe.

In the year 1850, the value of the exports and imports respectively did not exceed the sum of twenty-five million dollars. For many succeeding years the amount did not vary essentially from that sum. Thus, in 1875-76, the imports reached $28,485,000. The exports amounted to $25,435,000. Of the latter sum, fifteen millions consisted of silver.

During the fiscal year 1879-80, the value of the exports was $32,663,525, as follows:

To the United States	$13,416,600
" Great Britain	11,037,594
" France	5,194,741
" Germany	1,498,734
" Spain	1,009,368
" South America	506,488
Total	$32,663,525

One half of all the exports was shipped from the port of Vera Cruz.

The commercial marine comprises twelve hundred and sixty-eight vessels, of which number four hundred and twenty-one are employed in the foreign trade, and eight hundred and forty-seven in the coasting trade.

The absence of official, or other trustworthy data, renders it extremely difficult for the student of Mexican affairs to arrive at satisfactory conclusions. As regards the all-important matter of Education, I have abandoned the investigation of the subject in despair. Where the authorities are at variance with each other, I have chosen the one which appears to be best entitled to credit.

The following exhibits of the Public Debt and the Public Finances are taken from the *Almanach de Gotha*. They will serve to illustrate the fiscal embarrassments with which the present authorities have to contend.

THE PUBLIC DEBT.

1. Foreign debts................		$104,712,570
English debt of 14th Oct., 1850........	$89,252,360	
English Convention of 4th Dec., 1851....	5,900,025	
Spanish Convention of 6th Dec., 1853....	1,231,775	
Spanish Convention of 12th Nov., 1853...	5,553,287	
Indebtedness to the United States of 4th July, 1868......	2,775,123	
2. Internal debt................		40,241,215
Total...................		$144,953,785

It is to be borne in mind that this large aggregate is, for the most part, due to the injustice, the rapacity and hostility of other nations, and not to the lack of ability or integrity on the part of the Mexicans themselves.

THE FINANCES. (In dollars.)

Receipts.

	Budget 1882–83.
Custom-Houses	$15,000,000
Custom-House of Mexico and Excise	2,000,000
Stamps	4,000,000
Direct Tax	900,000
Mint	690,000
Receipts from former Fund for Public Education	60,000
Post-Offices and Telegraphs	650,000
Lotteries	800,000
Other Receipts	3,000,000
Total	$27,100,000
Receipts from the several States	7,500,000
Grand Total	$34,600,000

Expenditures.

Legislative Power	$1,071,712
Executive Power	48,832

Supreme Court...................	$389,554
Foreign Affairs..................	336,280
Interior........................	3,235,118
Justice, Public Education........	1,215,473
Public Works (*Fomento*)..........	7,551,683
Treasury........................	4,648,377
War and Navy...................	8,514,478
Total.....................	$27,011,507
Expenditures of the several States......................	7,500,000
Grand Total.............	$34,511,507

CHAPTER XII.

SAN JUAN TEOTIHUACAN.

LIKE the great pyramid of Cholula, to which they are accounted to be only second in antiquity, the celebrated prehistoric pyramids of San Juan Teotihuacan are objects of the highest interest. They are situated on the outskirts of the village of the same name, which is twenty-five miles distant from the capital. By starting from the City of Mexico, in the morning train of the Mexican Railway, ample time was afforded me to examine them, on all sides and in every part, and to return the same day. A walk of a little less than two miles from the railway station brings you to the site of these structures. The two principal ones are four-sided, facing the cardinal points of the compass, and are about half a mile distant from each other. According to an immemorial tradition, the larger one was dedicated to the Sun. In size, it is hardly inferior to the pyramid of Cheops on the plain of Ghizeh, being six hundred and eighty-two feet long at the base, with a height of one hundred and eighty feet. The smaller one was sacred to the Moon. Unlike the vast structure at Cholula, a large quantity of loose stones was used in their construction.

Originally, these pyramids each had four terraces; but I was able to distinguish only three. When first discovered by Europeans, some ruins were found on their summits; now nothing of the kind remains.

With a view to the determination of the long mooted question, whether they are hollow in their construction, M. Désiré Charnay, the enterprising explorer, whose name, in conjunction with that of Pierre Lorillard, Esq., has latterly been associated with the ruins of Mexico and Central America, has recently examined these pyramids. Although he discovered several recesses in the walls, and collected some relics from a place which he conjectured to be the tomb of a chief, the doubt as to whether they are solid or hollow still remains to be solved.

Besides the main structures referred to, there are many smaller ones, which are supposed to have been sacred to the stars. A dim and shadowy tradition, however, refers to these lesser *tumuli* as the graves of the nobles of the nation. Hence the plain on which they stand was called by the Aztecs *Micoatl*, the Path of the Dead.

To these pyramids, the spot owes the designation of *Teotihuacan*, the Dwelling-place of the Gods. It was once a great and flourishing city and the resort of myriads of devout pilgrims; but the introduction by the Spanish Conqueror of a new and purer faith, has, in the lapse of ages, led to its present decay.

In the temple which once stood upon the summit of the larger edifice was a statue of the presiding deity, the Sun. It was of a single block of stone and faced the east. A plate of burnished gold protected its heart, on which the first rays fell in the morning. That fiery soldier of the cross, Archbishop Zumarraga, in his zeal against pagan monuments, demolished it ; as he did every other symbol of the pre-Hispanic religion which came in his way.

A lively trade in Aztec and Toltec relics is carried on here by the natives. Some of the smaller articles which they offer for sale are probably genuine. Not so, however, with the large jars of pottery, ingeniously ornamented with hieroglyphics and o.her symbols, which they frequently succeed in palming off upon unsophisticated travellers. I was told that one of these was recently purchased by a stranger for the sum of thirty Mexican dollars, which the Curator of the National Museum, without a moment's hesitation, pronounced to be a counterfeit. I had the good fortune to buy one of the same description for the sum of seventy-five cents.

In past ages, the worship of the Sun, Moon, and Constellations has been practised by various races of men, and in widely different portions of the earth. Even in our day, it unquestionably prevails to some extent among the aborigines of the Western Hemisphere. Some of the old writers like Macrobius, who lived in the early part of the fifth century of the Christian era, have endeavored to prove that the principal divinities in all the heathen mythologies are personifications of the Sun. The myths of the Aztecs, and other races of both North and South America, are perhaps susceptible of this interpretation. It is, however, by no means certain that any of them regarded the material planet as being itself the divinity. In the infancy of language, they were compelled to employ words, derived from sensuous experience, to express ideas of a metaphysical character; as wind for spirit, light for truth, the hand for energy. As in metaphor, the containing vessel is named to denote the substance which it contains, so the Sun may have been made the religious symbol of the Supreme Being. Nezahualcoyatl, the sovereign of Tezcuco, we are told, reared a pyramid and placed on it a temple ten stories high which he dedicated to the Unknown God, the Cause of Causes. No image was placed in it, nor was blood ever shed there in worship—flowers and incense were the only offerings.

The Moon-Goddess was associated by the ancient inhabitants of Mexico with night, water, and production. She protected women and their babes, and blessed the rites of marriage. She caused the earth to yield its harvests; she sent the timely rain; but she was capricious and hard to please. Night, damp and cold were her ministers, and fevers, pain and death proceeded from her. Contained in their baptismal formula were the words: "We are all under the power of evil and sin, because we are the children of the Water." Hence to propitiate her was an essential office of the Aztec ritual. "The Moon was worshipped as the wife of the Sun," says the historian Veytia, "and the Stars as his sisters." The Toltecs everywhere associated them in their rites, and regarded them as the abode of souls. Like the Vedic Aryans, and like the Greeks of a remote antiquity, they worshipped the Sky, or the God of Heaven, as the Over-lord of the Universe, and they venerated the wind as his Spirit. The Sun, Moon, Planets and Constellations were regarded as the subordinate representations of these supreme powers in their various specific manifestations. "I have always pictured to myself our Areskui" (meaning the Sun and Supreme Being), said a Huron woman, " as of the same nature which you ascribe to your God."

The Natchez and other aborigines regarded the Sun as the great fire, and so worshipped it as the source of life. "The life in your body and the fire on your hearth are one, and from the same source," said a Shawnee chief. "The ancient God, the Father and Mother of all Gods," says an Aztec prayer, "is the God of the Fire." General J. M. Brown writes that the Blackfeet Indians, in every instance when questioned, explained that they prayed, not to the Sun, but to the Old Man (*quære*, the Great Spirit?) who lives there. This corresponds exactly with the Septuagint version of the words of the Hebrew Psalmist: "He hath set His tabernacle in the sun." Neither the Hebrew nor the American considered the symbol or dwelling-place as identical with the dweller in it.

Thus the religion represented by the pyramids at San Juan Teotihuacan would seem to have been but a variation of other primeval world-wide faiths. It associated physical phenomena with invisible power; it was neither monotheism, pantheism, nor fetishism, but, as Kant has expressed it, a conviction of a highest and first principle, which binds all phenomena into one.

That the Aztecs recognized one Supreme Lord of the Universe, there is little room to doubt. They addressed Him in their prayers as "the God by whom we live"; "omnipresent"; "that knoweth all thoughts and giveth all gifts"; "without whom man is as nothing"; "invisible, incorporeal, one God, of perfect perfection and purity"; "under whose wings we find repose and a sure defence." At the same time they recognized a plurality of deities, who presided over the elements, the changes of the seasons, and the various occupations of men. Of these, there were thirteen principal deities, and more than two hundred inferior, to each of whom some special day or appropriate festival was consecrated. We search the Aztec theology in vain for those doctrines which constitute the crowning glory of Christianity, and which serve to reconcile us to time, by proving it to be but the transparent veil of eternity.

CHAPTER XIII.

ASCENT OF THE GREAT VOLCANO.

It had long been my purpose, before leaving home, to visit the most celebrated volcanoes of Mexico. The principal of these, the famous volcano of Popocatepetl, is now the property of General Gaspar Sanchez Ochoa. This distinguished gentleman was in active service during the war with the French, and commanded the national forces in the State of Puebla. President Juarez afterwards intrusted him with a confidential mission to our Government. It was my good fortune to obtain a formal introduction to him. I was not only graciously accorded permission to ascend the mountain, but the General with the utmost courtesy gave me a letter of commendation to his superintendent at Amecameca, a town near the base of the mountain.

General Ochoa expressed his opinions with soldierly frankness in regard to political matters.

Neither the Americans nor Mexicans, he warmly declared, would ever tolerate a king or emperor. The Mexicans had found it necessary, when Maximilian attempted to establish a military despotism on their soil, to shoot him, as they had before done with the Emperor Iturbide. He cherished, he said, a grateful remembrance of the intervention of the United States in behalf of his country, and he gratefully acknowledged its great value. Nevertheless he had no doubt that the Mexicans alone would, in time, have expelled the French from their soil.

Popocatepetl, meaning in the Aztec language "The Mountain that Smokes," is, according to the observations of Baron von Humboldt, seventeen thousand seven hundred and twenty feet in height. Later observations, however, have assigned to the great volcano a height of seventeen thousand eight hundred and fifty-two feet. It is nearly three times the height of Mount Washington, the highest of the White Mountains, and over two thousand feet higher than Mont Blanc, in Switzerland. Iztaccihuatl, another volcano, stands in close proximity to it.

The name signifies "White Woman," and tradition represents Popocatepetl as being the monarch of the mountains, and Iztaccihuatl as his wife.

The ascent of Popocatepetl is a formidable undertaking. It is seldom made except by the peons who are employed in the crater. General Ochoa derives a considerable income from the sulphur obtained from that source. I made the ascent in company with my brother, who, having trodden nearly all of the loftiest pinnacles of the Alps, was well qualified by his experience to undertake the ascent of the grandest mountain of this continent. The volcano is fifty miles from the capital, and is reached by way of the Morelos Railway to Amecameca. Here we spent the night, and in the morning were furnished two guides by the superintendent referred to, who also gave us the key of the Rancho de Tlamacas, a hut in the mountains where we could pass the night.

Several days are required to make the ascent, and the severest physical exertion, personal risk, exposure and hardship, must inevitably be en-

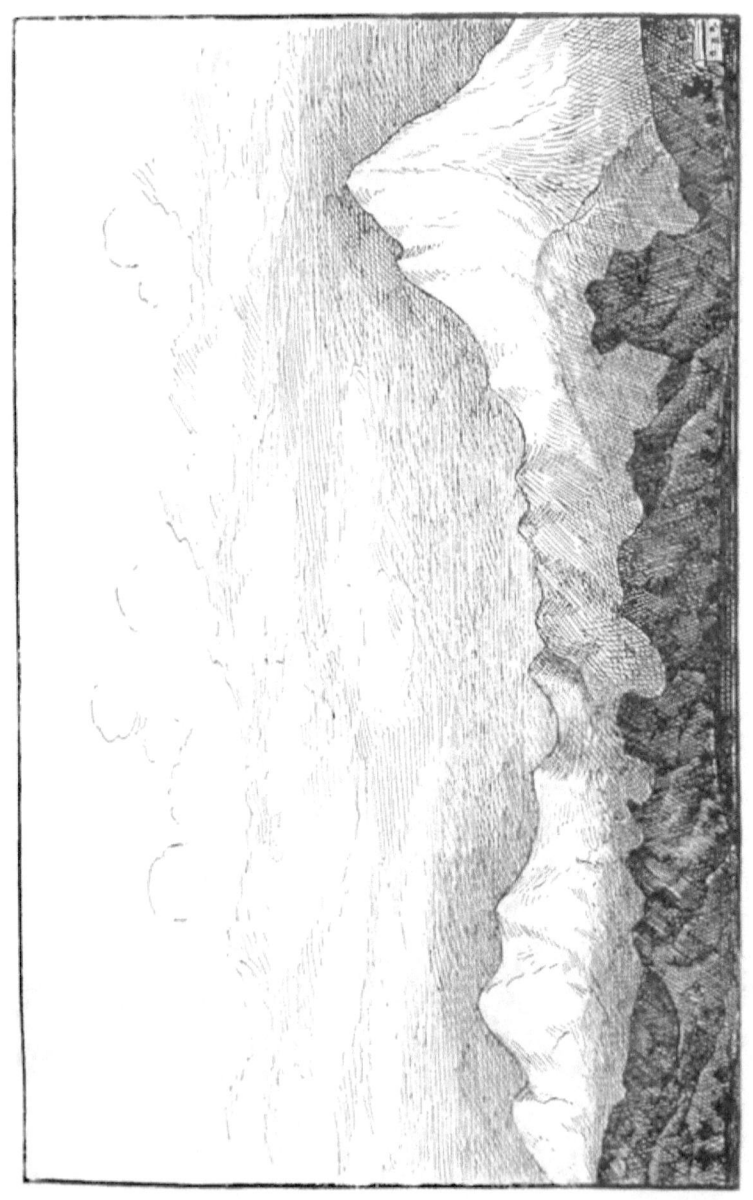

IZTACCIHUATL. POPOCATEPETL.

From a pen and ink sketch by the Author.

countered. The preliminary arrangements will be attended with many annoying delays, as the people do not like to hurry themselves, and must have a little time to think over every proposition which is made to them. Upon speaking to the hotel proprietor about our plans, he obtained for us a middleman, there being many of these in Mexico, who engaged to furnish horses and attend us in person. So, taking provisions for two days, blankets and other necessary articles, we set out at two o'clock one afternoon for Tlamacas, which is situated at a distance of twelve miles from the foot of the mountain. At first the region which we traversed was fertile and beautiful; next came splendid timber-lands; farther on, tall, sombre pines, growing in a wilderness of rank, coarse grass, and then came that scantiness of vegetation which is incident to all high altitudes. At seven in the evening we had arrived at the ranch, about thirteen thousand five hundred feet above the sea-level, and only a short distance below the line of perpetual snow. It was a hut used by the peons who transport the sulphur on their backs; but this being Holy Week, and, of course, a holiday time, they were away. We picketed our horses, and, entering the cabin, built a fire in the middle of the earthen floor, after the true Indian style. There was no chimney, but numerous gaps and crevices in the roof and walls gave abundant egress to the smoke. After a cold supper we lay down to sleep on some bare planks, wrapped in our blankets, taking care, however, to keep our revolvers within convenient distance. From time to time, during the night, one of the party would rise and replenish the fire. This was indispensable to our comfort, as the piercing wind, blowing down from the region of eternal snow and ice, made its way into the hut on every side.

At half-past three in the morning we rose and prepared to ascend the cone. I wore an ordinary heavy business-suit, with canvas leggings and shoes purchased for the occasion. A large straw hat, a havelock, and a pair of green goggles were worn for protection against the direct rays of the sun and the reflection from the snow. A pair of mittens, an alpenstock, and a small flannel hat stuck into a belt completed my outfit. One of the guides carried a knapsack with provisions. The horses were left at the ranch, and we set out, on foot, at half-past four o'clock in the morning. The full moon shone brightly, and we walked rapidly in Indian file through a very wild region, where we could see the tracks of wolves in the sand and hear them baying in the distance. There was something weird in the sighing of the night wind through the leafless branches of the forest. After walking a mile we came to the snow. From this point our labors became very severe. We went up very steep inclines, through snow often knee-deep, for about fifteen hundred feet. Nowhere was the slope gradual enough to admit of a moment's relaxation.

We now came to a vast wall, almost perpendicular, of hard, frozen snow, which stretched upward for over twenty-five hundred feet to a point which the guides declared was the summit. The snow was so hard as to afford no foothold, thus adding inconceivably to our labor and peril. It would be impossible to say how far one would slide in case of a fall, except that the higher he had ascended the greater of course would be the descent. One of the guides went forward, and with a sharp spade cut steps in the snow, which made the ascent safer. Still the walking was very fatiguing. Making a zig-zag track he led the way up the great wall to places where those who are inclined to vertigo should be careful not to look down. Soon a strong sulphurous odor was perceptible, and increased in intensity with each successive step, until at length it became exceedingly oppressive.

When I was still about two thousand feet from the summit, I began to experience the effects peculiar to a highly rarefied atmosphere. Keeping on five hundred feet higher, I was almost prostrated. I experienced drowsiness, a peculiar clicking and singing sensation in the ears, accelerated breathing, palpitation of the heart, and violent headache. My brother, however, experienced none of these inconveniences, and reached the summit nearly two hours before I did, almost as fresh as when he set out. These sensations, so often affecting mountain-climbers, are not by any means due to the lack of muscular power, but to inability to breathe comfortably in such rarefied air. The strongest man in the world might fail to reach the summits of comparatively low mountains, if his lungs were not suited to breathing air of this kind. By a strong effort of the will, I was at length able to reach the top of the mountain at about a quarter of an hour before noon, having walked, without intermission, seven hours and a quarter since leaving the hut. I made the last two hundred feet over needle-like points of ice, with every certainty of going thousands of feet without stopping, in case of a slip or a false step.

Utterly exhausted, I threw myself on the ground just inside of the edge of the crater, where I was partially sheltered from the fierceness of the wind. My brother made me as comfortable as possible under the circumstances, supplying me with dry shoes and socks, which had been brought up in the knapsack for the purpose. After dozing for a short time I was somewhat revived, and was able to get up and take a view of the surroundings.

The summit has a very small superficial area, owing to the immense crater that meets the eye the moment the last upward step is taken. The crater is very deep, the guides say five hundred feet, but probably it is much more. The walls are very steep, steam issues with a puffing sound from various fissures, and numerous yellow masses indicate the presence of sulphur. At the bottom of the crater is a pool of clear water of a greenish hue, but I had neither the time, means, nor inclination to descend the precipitous sides and investigate the cause of its singular color.

The Spaniards, in the earlier periods of their occupation of the country, here procured sulphur for the manufacture of gunpowder, but there has been some difference of opinion among historians, whether the Spaniards took the sulphur from the crater or from some crevice in the side of the mountain, which was in a state of eruption at about that period.

In the early morning, the valleys had been

covered by heavy clouds. The rising of the sun over them was a glorious sight, easier to imagine than to describe. Presently they began to rise, revealing the beauties of the Valley of Amecameca and of the great Valley of Mexico. The City of Puebla and the pyramid of Cholula were distinctly visible. The clouds approached nearer and nearer, and at last began to gather around us. The guides, at this moment, with evident signs of apprehension, urged us to set out at once upon our return. The wind was terrific, and when we were again on the icy snow there was danger of being thrown down by it. Accordingly, that I might present less surface, I gave my large hat to the guide and put on the small one. Of course I suffered the penalty— my face being blistered by the direct and reflected rays of the sun.

When the most dangerous places had been passed, the guides each took a palm-leaf mat from their backs and suggested coasting. This seemed very dangerous, but it was undoubtedly the quickest way of getting down, and as every step I made was attended, exhausted as I was, with great effort and even pain, I decided to try it. I sat down behind one of them, and away we went down the steep incline, making about five hundred feet at a time. In the early hours of the day, when the snow remained hard, from the influence of the low temperature of the night, this would have been nothing short of foolhardy, but it was now past noon, and the snow had been softened by the heat of the sun. We could stop at intervals by selecting for the purpose some particularly soft spot, or by putting our alpenstocks behind and throwing our weight upon them, at the same instant burying our heels in the snow. After the novelty wore off we resumed walking, and arrived at the ranch in about two hours, when we immediately commenced preparations for returning to the plain. We proceeded to disencumber ourselves of the articles for which we had no farther use, and presented hats, leggings, shoes, a lantern and other articles to the guides. It being no doubt the first time they had ever experienced such a wind-fall, they seemed very grateful. Finding our liberality continue, beyond any expected limits, they became emboldened to ask for still other articles, which we were not prepared to surrender.

We were soon ready to start, and mounting our horses, we descended the mountain by the very route taken by the Conqueror, when he first led his army into the Valley of Tenochtitlan.

The guide left in charge of the horses had neglected to fasten one of them securely, and he had strayed home. Consequently, the man was obliged to walk, but I finally took pity on him and let him get on behind me, and in this manner we rode into the town of Amecameca, arriving at eight in the evening—the day being Good Friday. The town was filled to overflowing with country people, and a grand torch-light procession was in progress. The people lay asleep in dense rows under the trees in the public square, and in every other available spot. They could not afford to pay for beds, nor, as far as I could judge, did they desire them. In walking, it was necessary to use some precaution to avoid stepping on some sleeper. When we applied for accommodations at a hotel—not the one at which we had stopped before—the landlady, evidently taking into consideration the character of stray travellers in general, regarded us with considerable suspicion, and demanded and received payment in advance for her rooms. In the morning, the peons and their families besieged the station an hour and a half before train time, all going into the capital to spend the holidays. Many of them, probably, had never ridden on a railroad train before. The train was of great length, and platform and freight cars were pressed into service for their accommodation. Every station swelled the number of passengers, and when the train entered the station of San Lazaro, the population of the metropolis was temporarily increased by some thousands of souls.

I have thus dwelt, perhaps at too great length, upon the details and incidents of this enterprise, for the reason that, in looking back upon it, I am unable to perceive in what manner the preparations for it, which were made by my brother, could have been in any particular improved. Hence I advise those who may hereafter attempt the ascent of the great volcano, to imitate my example in this regard. Another and more important reason has prompted me. The ascent of Popocatepetl, notwithstanding its cost in time, labor, and money, will be a memorable event in the life of any tourist. The vastness and sublimity of the field of vision which its summit commands, cannot fail forever to stand out in conspicuous relief among his choicest memories.

CHAPTER XIV.

QUERETARO.—MR. SEWARD'S VISIT.

Although I had passed several weeks in the capital, and had been so busily engaged as hardly to allow myself time for needed rest, I reluctantly came away without visiting several localities of historical importance, and without studying various objects of interest which are peculiar to the Land of the Aztecs. Having resolved to return home by the overland route, I decided to make the tour of the principal cities in the Northern States, with San Luis Potosi as my objective point. A line of diligences is run from that city to Monterey, and there connects with the Mexican National Railway, the terminus of which is Laredo, on the Rio Grande.

Candor compels me to say that this route is attended with numerous inconveniences. Whether you start from Queretaro or Lagos, it involves seven successive days of diligence travel from four o'clock in the morning until six o'clock in the evening. At present the latter place is the temporary terminus of the Mexican Central Railroad.

The route which I decided to take, by way of the City of Zacatecas, involves nine days of diligence travel. One day is certain to be lost on the route, as, throughout Mexico, Monday is always a day of rest on all diligence lines. Then, the diligence is run but three times a week, setting out, as has been stated, on each successive day of the journey at four in the morning. Should the seats be all engaged, at least two days, if not more, must be lost while waiting for a vacancy to occur. In addition to the discomforts of rising at an unreasonably early hour on so many consecutive days, the hotel accommodations are everywhere inferior, and are not unfrequently insufficient to meet the demands of the public. During the hours of travel the opportunities for getting meals occur at irregular intervals, while the quality of the food is, at best, far from palatable.

The train on the Mexican Central Railroad, which leaves the capital at a quarter after six o'clock in the morning, gives the passengers five minutes for coffee at one of the small stations on the route. A stop is made for a mid-day breakfast at San Juan del Rio, where the fare in the railroad restaurant is in all respects unexceptionable.

I left the train at the important and beautiful City of Queretaro. On account of the number of her spires, our youthful neighbor, Brooklyn, has been named the "The City of Churches"; but she is poor in the proportion which her religious edifices bear to the aggregate of her population in comparison to Queretaro, with her almost countless domes and towers (spires not being used in the church architecture of Mexico).

The streets are clean, and the parks are tastefully embellished. The *Alameda*, the largest and most attractive of these, is a delightful pleasure ground, where the shade of the trees offers the weary a charming retreat. An abundant supply of good drinking water is brought into the city by means of a long aqueduct, which was built a century ago.

The Hotel de Diligencias is fairly well kept, and the galleries in the court-yard are adorned with exquisite roses growing in handsome flower-pots. The air is salubrious. The site of the city is less elevated than that of the capital, consequently the flowers are even more beautiful and abundant.

The city is celebrated for its connection with the later history of Maximilian. After the French armies had been withdrawn from the country, he retired with his forces from the capital and established himself here, relying, no doubt, on the well-known devotion of the people of Queretaro to the interests of the Church party. On the nineteenth day of May, 1867, as has been elsewhere stated, he was made a prisoner, and, after a trial by court-martial, was shot, with two of his officers. I walked out to the spot where he died, at the hour of sunset, on Easter Sunday. The day had been one of remarkable beauty, and the gorgeous coloring of the western sky added to the beauties of a lovely and picturesque landscape. Standing on the slight eminence which rises from a fertile plain, whose stately trees and splendid fields of grain border the fair city, which was gilded by the last rays of the setting sun, with surroundings so peaceful and picturesque, I could hardly realize that this had been the theatre on which the dark tragedy had been enacted, which put an end to one of the blackest crimes which history has recorded.

The "Hercules" cotton-mill is one of the lions at Queretaro. It is situated two and a half miles from the city, in a deep *cañon*, and is the most extensive establishment of the kind in the country. It began operations in 1840, and gives employment to fourteen hundred hands at its looms. The machinery is of the best quality and of the most improved patterns. Both steam and water power are used. The former drives an engine of one hundred and fifty horse-power, and the latter turns an overshot wheel forty-six feet in diameter. The cost of construction was four million dollars. The operatives employed are Indians, there being about as many women as men. The wages of the common hands are about thirty-seven and a half cents a day, Mexican money. Four Englishmen act as foremen, and each receives a compensation of four dollars a day.

The buildings are of stone, and have the unique accompaniment of fine gardens containing artificial ponds. Here are orange-trees laden with fruit, peach-trees, figs and pomegranates. Roses, geraniums, fuchsias and numerous tropical flowers also abound. A statue of Hercules, executed in Italy, and other works of art adorn the place.

A wall pierced for musketry encloses the several buildings, and a squad of thirty soldiers in uniform is always on duty. This precaution is thought to be necessary on account of the frequent revolutions and uprisings which, in the past, have characterized Mexican history. On such occasions lawless individuals turn out in gangs, and under various pretexts break open houses and plunder everything which they can lay hands upon. A similar exhibition of violence and robbery, it will be remembered, was witnessed in the City of New York in the celebrated riots of July, 1863. The mills are well guarded against such outbreaks. An arsenal attached to them is well supplied with Remington rifles, swords, revolvers and howitzers. Every appliance that is necessary to give a fitting reception to marauding visitors of the character referred to is here provided.

I found the proprietor exceedingly polite and affable. He is the son of the first owner and founder of the establishment, Don Francisco Rubio, and is himself one of the most active, enterprising and enlightened men in Mexico. He possesses an extraordinary endowment of nervous energy, and talks with the greatest animation. He informed me that he made a journey to England for the express purpose of learning the business in the mills of Manchester, returning home in 1856. He has superintended the works ever since his return.

He spoke very highly of the Indian operatives and their great powers of endurance. When I was there the mill was running on extra time, and the hands were kept at work from half-past five in the morning till half-past nine at night, a half hour only being allowed them for breakfast and an hour for dinner. There had been but one strike during twenty-six years. Two hundred operatives then refused to work, and he, in turn, refused to employ them a second time. They threatened his life, but he armed himself and would not give way to intimidation.

The Governor of the State of Queretaro, fearing the consequences of his determined stand, finally visited him and demanded that he should permit the strikers to resume work. He simply answered: "If you will come and take charge of the mill they can return; but on the day that the first one comes, I will go." Of course his Excellency could not agree to this. He then added: "If you will attend to your business I will attend to mine."

On the very first day that he went abroad unarmed, a man came up to him with hat in hand as though as he were humbly asking for work. As soon, however, as he had approached near enough, the miscreant suddenly drew a knife and inflicted a dangerous wound, making his escape immediately afterward.

The people of Queretaro hold in grateful, indeed I may say affectionate, remembrance, the visit which the Hon. William H. Seward, accompanied by Mr. and Mrs. Frederick W. Seward, paid to their city, toward the close of the year 1869. It will be remembered that, soon after that gentleman's retirement from the office of Secretary of State, the Mexican authorities intimated a wish that he would at an early period favor them with his presence. Accordingly, in the autumn of the year 1869, after a brief sojourn in the City of San Francisco, he took passage on board "The Golden City" steamer, for Manzanillo on the Pacific coast, where, with his suite, he was landed in the month of October— the people turning out *en masse* to welcome him.

From that port to the City of Mexico his journey assumed the character of a triumphal progress. He was everywhere hailed with the most enthusiastic demonstrations of popular respect and gratitude, as "*El Ilustre Americano*," who had done so much to uphold the Republic when its life was menaced by foreign invasion; and to whose interposition Mexico was so largely indebted for the victory which at last crowned her struggle for independence.

The second grand ovation in his honor took place at the City of Colima, the capital of the State of the same name. Here the Governor, in a graceful and eloquent speech, welcomed him to a grand ball and banquet.

Mr. Seward's response was worthy of his high renown as a statesman and orator. It was printed in the Spanish language, and was circulated in all parts of the country. The generous and lofty sentiments to which he gave utterance, in the light of subsequent events seem almost prophetic. I cannot resist the temptation to add both interest and value to my narrative by here inserting it in its entirety. Mr. Seward spoke as follows:

GENTLEMEN:

I thank you with a full heart for these and all the other distinguished hospitalities and honors which have been showered upon me in this respected and ancient capital of Colima.

The experience of the 18th century indicated to mankind two important changes of society and government on the continent of America. First, that all American States must thereafter be, not dependent European colonies, but independent native American nations. Second, that all independent American nations must thereafter have, not imperial or monarchial governments, but republican governments, constituted and carried on by the voluntary agency of the people themselves.

During a large part of my own political life, these great changes of society and government have been more or less contested—in logical debate in Europe and on the battle-field throughout America. While they have often involved the American States in civil and international wars, they have more than once provoked European intervention.

A third improvement was early found necessary to guarantee success to the two principal changes which I have already mentioned. This third improvement consists in the combination of the many or several contiguous States, which are weak of themselves, into distinct nations.

My own country, the United States, has taken the lead in these changes, so essential in the American hemisphere.

The Mexican Republic has, bravely and persistently, adopted a similar system. Central America, and nearly all the South American States, have followed the example thus set by the United States and by the Mexican Republic. One additional principle remains to be adopted to secure the success of the republican system throughout the continent. If it shall become universal on the American continent, we have reason to expect that the same great system may be accepted by other nations throughout the world. That additional principle is simply this, that the several American Republics, just as they constitute themselves, while mutually abstaining from intervention with each other, shall become, more than ever heretofore, political friends through the force of moral alliance.

This, in short, is the policy which I have inculcated at home, and which, with your leave, and the leave of others interested, I shall commend as far as possible to the Republics of Mexico, Central America, and South America.

I sincerely trust that the severest trials of the republican system are already passed in Mexico; and I shall never cease to pray God for her continued independence, unity, prosperity and happiness.

Having spent some time at Queretaro, Mr. Seward proceeded by slow stages to the capital. At a distance of two miles from the city he was met by President Juarez, Señor Lerdo De Tejada, the Minister of Foreign Relations, Minister Romero, Hon. Thomas H. Nelson, United States Minister to Mexico, and an escort of about four hundred soldiers. The reception was enthusiastic, and the greetings extended to the distinguished American were extremely gratifying to him. He was conducted in all the pomp of military display to the capital; and was there formally installed in one of the handsomest houses in the city, which had been especially prepared for his accommodation. He was here bidden to make himself perfectly at home during his stay at the capital, and the freedom of the city was heartily extended to him.

A round of magnificent entertainments and festivities, lasting through many days, now followed each other in rapid succession. Similar ovations and honors followed him all the way to the City of Vera Cruz, where he embarked for the United States. In variety, in extent and splendor, the tributes rendered to Mr. Seward far surpassed those ever paid to any other foreigner by the people of our sister Republic.

When Mexico shall finally make up her jewels, his effigy may be assigned a place, in her National Pantheon, beside that of Washington.

CHAPTER XV.

THE NORTHERN CITIES.

I REMAINED at Queretaro till the afternoon of Easter Monday, and then resumed my journey. The region through which I now passed was even more beautiful than that which I had just traversed. Occasionally, however, the railroad intersects a district where only the cactus flourishes. The variety which appears on the national coat-of-arms is a feature of nearly every landscape in Mexico. There are many genera and species of cacti recognized by botanists. The cereus grows here, including the night-blooming variety, the *Bonplandii* and others now used in medicine. The organ cactus is most highly esteemed by the Mexicans. It was so named from its resemblance to the pipes of a church organ. It is frequently planted on the lines bounding separate estates, and serves the purpose of a fence.

I passed the towns of Celaya, Salamanca and other neat and orderly places. At Silao, I took the branch line for the City of Guanajuato. The terminus of this branch road is at Marfil, three miles before Guanajuato is reached. This distance is accomplished by stage or tramway. The road passes through a deep and narrow gorge of the mountain, at the extremity of which the city lies.

Guanajuato is the capital of the State of that name, and is a flourishing city with about sixty thousand inhabitants. Situated as it is at the termination of a ravine, the streets are not regularly laid out as in other towns, but are eccentric in their respective courses, like those of the older part of Boston.

Some of the richest silver mines in the world are found in the hills surrounding the city, and it owes to them its chief importance. Humboldt estimated that they produced one-fifth of the silver of the world. Their present yield is about five million dollars a year. The metal is extracted by the *patio* or cold amalgamation process, which is explained in the chapter on

Mining; but the pioneer steam stamping-mill has been erected, and others are certain to follow.

The spirit of the age appears to have reached the inhabitants of this old, conservative town. They seem to be almost universally engaged in learning the English language, as though in anticipation of the period soon to arrive when this knowledge will be indispensable. I observed a barber, on the other side of the street from the hotel where I was sojourning. He studied all day long, walking to and fro in his shop, and conning the sentences of a conversation-book. I imagine that he will soon be able to entertain his American patrons with the news of the day, and with dissertations on art, science, literature and ethics, on a par with any German barber in the City of New York.

The telephone has come. An American company has already established branches in the principal cities, and there are seventy-five instruments in use in Guanajuato.

The prison is a well-regulated institution, and is noticeable both for its dimensions and from the absence of windows on the exterior. It was the last place in the State of Guanajuato which the Spaniards were able to hold in the war for Mexican independence. They retreated to it and strongly fortified themselves. Their Indian assailants, who were destitute of fire-arms, suffered severely from the Spanish bullets. They, however, improvised a protection against these by carrying flat stones on their shoulders, which were large enough to cover their heads. In this manner, stooping over so that their entire bodies might be shielded, they made their way to the gate, in defiance of the musketry of the besieged soldiers, and set it on fire. It is related that four chiefs fell into the hands of the Spaniards, who cut off their heads and hung them on nails on each corner of the doorway.

The stage-coach and mule-cars leave the city every afternoon to meet the railway trains. They generally race all the way. The former vehicle is driven in the most reckless manner through the crowds of idlers who forever stand in the middle of the principal thoroughfares; but somehow they manage to get out of the way in time to escape being run down. The cars have the better of it at the start, but the stage-coach takes a short cut, and by driving down a steep and stony hill at a furious pace, dashes up to the station and secures the first place.

In taking the branch road back to Silao, it was necessary for me to wait forty minutes for the train going northward. There is a restaurant near the station, where I found it pleasant to wait. The Frenchman who keeps it has achieved a wide reputation in all this region for the excellence of his *menu*.

The ride on the railroad was a pleasant one. At nightfall I reached Lagos, which is the present terminus of the railroad. There is little of note about this town. The diligence hotel is not equal to the Fifth Avenue Hotel, but still it is comfortable. Yet the arrangements admit of improvement. When I left my room at four the next morning to take the diligence, I was obliged to go through the apartments of several other guests, or "passengers," as they are called. The vehicle was almost full of travellers, three of whom were women. In accordance with the custom of the country they wore no bonnets.

When the road is smooth enough to permit it, everybody goes to sleep in these early rides, except the driver, and he barely keeps awake. When a passenger purchases his ticket, a seat is assigned to him, as he may select, and its number is written on the ticket. Nobody, however, pays any attention to this. The wary and experienced *voyageur* comes early to the coach, seats himself in the best place that he can find, and goes quietly to sleep. After several hours, when the sun is up, every one awakes, and all become sociable.

The road from Lagos is sandy for a considerable distance, and very promotive of repose. Presently, however, came a hilly district which was fearfully rough and stony. The driver appealed to his passengers: "Would they do him the favor to walk a little way?" All complied without hesitation. After six hours a stop was made for refreshment. It was a poor-looking place, but the repast was excellent. The road beyond this point extended thirty-five miles through a level region, which, like most of the *Tierras Frias* of Northern Mexico, is destitute of trees. Indian corn is successfully cultivated here, and much of the land is devoted to grazing.

Late in the afternoon I came to the City of *Aguas Calientes*, or Hot Springs, the capital of the State of that name. It derives its name from the thermal waters that are found there. The inhabitants number about thirty-five thousand.

It loses nothing by a comparison with its American namesake — that wretched hamlet which has sprung up amid the wilds of Arkansas, where all is noise and bustle, and where bands of music play at the railroad station when the trains arrive.

The City of Aguas Calientes is in direct and admirable contrast. Here everything is quiet and orderly. The streets are wide and clean, and there are parks in abundance, well supplied with beautiful flowers. In one of them there is a monument to Hidalgo.

At the springs extensive and commodious bathing-houses have been erected, which are surrounded with flower gardens.

The city contains thirteen churches, a hospital, a penitentiary for women, and a jail.

At a recent bull-fight in this place, the Committee of Arrangements invited four young ladies, two Mexican and two American, to be present and act as queens. The Mexicans accepted, but, strange to say, only one of the Americans complied with the flattering request.

The Hotel de Diligencias at Aguas Calientes is a well kept inn. When travelling in the interior of the country I have found it the wiser course to stop at the diligence hotels, as the stages always leave very early in the morning and it is much more convenient to be on the spot. Besides, coffee is served before setting out, which is not the case at other hotels. Many of them are owned, or at least controlled, by the Diligence Company, and are therefore apt to be better managed than those the proprietors of which have less capital at command.

One of the hotels in which I was a guest was kept by a fine-looking, intelligent and well-educated man, who was evidently fitted for a far higher kind of employment. I learned that he had been a priest, and was highly regarded by those with whom he came in contact. It was found out, however, that he was an inveterate gambler, and was bringing scandal upon the Church by his conduct. Accordingly, his superiors, very justly and to their own honor, removed him from holy orders.

The journey in the diligence from Aguas Calientes was through similar scenes to those which I had witnessed on the preceding days. I passed through a number of forlorn little villages, with houses built of *adobe*, or sun-dried brick, looking to be the very embodiment of wretchedness itself. My fellow-passengers were chiefly Americans. One of them was an itinerant dentist, who entertained me with a rather prolonged discourse in relation to the demand for artificial teeth in the Mexican market. He proved, however, to be a good fellow at bottom, or it may be that I became accustomed to his peculiarities. Byron says:—

> " My very chains and I grew friends;
> So much a long communion tends
> To make us what we are."

At noon I arrived at a little town called El Rincon de Roma, and a few minutes later I brought up at a superior *hacienda*. The water supply in this part of the central table-land is very limited. At this place it is obtained from a neighboring hill a mile and a half distant, by means of a stone aqueduct, and is stored here in a large reservoir.

The plain as I advanced became more and more narrow, and the road was rough and broken. Some hills which I passed were so uniform in their contour as to present the appearance of having been artificially constructed.

The town of Guadalupe is situated four miles from Zacatecas, of which it is in fact a suburb. Their interests are identical, and the places are connected by a line of cars which runs through the narrow *cañon* which lies between them. They are drawn up the ascending ground by mules; but as Zacatecas is six hundred feet higher than Guadalupe, no power is required on the return trip. The conductor uses the brake when the cars go too fast. Some persons doing business at Zacatecas prefer to live at the other town because it is of a lower altitude, and they find the atmosphere somewhat less rarefied. Hence the travel between the two places is considerable. In 1880, during the six months from May to October inclusive, the number of passengers on this road was one hundred and seventy-two thousand. The right of way is owned by the Mexican Central Railroad Company. They intend to run trains over it when they have completed their main line.

Zacatecas was constituted a city by a decree of Philip II. of Spain, in 1685. It is situated in a ravine, and is surrounded on every side by barren mountains. The streets are very uneven, constantly ascending and descending, and are otherwise diversified. Instead of being paved with rough cobble-stone, as elsewhere, many of them are macadamized. Though surrounded with unfavorable environments, Zacatecas is a very pleasant city, well built, clean and healthy. It has, however, a deficient supply of water. Many foreigners live here who are engaged in business relating to the mines. The State is regarded as the first in Mexico as regards mineral wealth. Gold, silver, lead, copper, and iron are produced.

The territory remained in possession of the Chichemecs until about three centuries ago, when it was overrun by the Spaniards. They worked the mines, and removed much of the ore lying near the surface. Many of them were then abandoned. The working of several of them has of late years been resumed, but the miners are now obliged to go to a great depth, which causes a serious drawback to the profits. The mine of San Rafael has a shaft eight hundred and fifty-six feet deep, and the descent is made by means of ladders. The old methods are still in vogue, and in many of the mines the peons carry up the ore on their backs. These men work many hours to the day, yet they receive only about one-fourth of the pay of white laborers in the United States.

There are eighteen mining districts in this State. The San Martin mine has a shaft seven hundred feet in depth, and the ore is raised to the surface in cars drawn up by steam power. These cars are also used by the miners to go into and come out from the mine. A mine once owned by Cortez was abandoned a few years ago, because its proprietors had no means of taking out the water, which, even in that particularly dry region, seems to abound in the shafts of mines. The inquiry constantly suggested itself, why not sink artesian wells to obtain a supply of water?

An Englishman, who uses the *patio* process, has a superior stamping-mill, which he has owned for upward of twenty years. He is very courteous, and tourists visiting this region will be amply repaid for examining his works.

The principal buildings of Zacatecas are the State House, city hall, cathedral, markets, hospital, jail, theatre, mint, and last but not least, the amphitheatre, where the bull-fights take place. The cathedral is noticeable for the fine carving of its brown-stone façade. The interior of the building exhibits the peculiar effects incident to white and gilt.

The Hotel Zacatecano is an excellent and well-conducted public house. The building was formerly a convent, and was purchased, together with the chapel, by the present owner after the sequestration of church property. He fitted it up and improved it, so that it is now a valuable and handsome property.

The former chapel of the convent is now occupied by the Presbyterian Mission. I attended the Sunday morning service. The congregation numbered about four hundred persons. The clergyman was an Italian, and a man of decided ability. His wife was a lady from Pittsburgh. The service was conducted in the Spanish language. The singing by the choir was very good— the congregation participating, but not with equal skill. Many of those present belonged to the poorest class, and worked for very low wages; yet when the plate was carried around, almost every one made a contribution. Their dress and personal appearance denoted a commendable degree of cleanliness and respectability.

I took the opportunity to make the acquaintance of the clergyman. He gave me an interesting history of the Mission. There would be, he assured me, a larger congregation at the evening service, usually about seven hundred. Sunday morning was a time for active business everywhere, and many found it difficult to attend worship at that time.

When the enterprise was inaugurated there were many obstacles to be encountered. The owner of the Hotel Zacatecano, a gentleman of progressive views, had generously provided the chapel, charging a rent which was merely nominal. The room was occupied, at the time, as a stable and ten-pin alley, and required alteration. The Roman Catholic bishop threatened with excommunication every mechanic and laborer who should dare to engage in the work. The State Government, however, which is liberal in its views, extended its aid, and offered the use of the convict laborers, with a company of soldiers to protect them while so employed. Thus the building was fitted up at an outlay of three thousand dollars. It is a comfortable, and even an attractive, place of worship.

The outlook for Protestant missions in this part of Mexico he considered to be very encouraging. The early impediments have been overcome, and there are twenty-two congregations now worshipping in the districts of Zacatecas, San Luis Potosi and Durango. All of them belong to the Presbyterian denomination.

While I remained at Zacatecas, the ball of the season took place. It was a grand occasion, but no Americans, except residents, were invited. The reason of this omission was said to be the rude conduct of several railroad men at the last ball. In order to prevent a repetition of their ruffianism, the committee of arrangements had decided to invite no Americans whose presence in the city was merely temporary.

Zacatecas is a great centre of travel. Lines of diligences enter it from every direction. One proprietor runs a wagon-train for the conveyance of both passengers and treasure northward to Monterey. He sets out with several vehicles and a drove of sixty mules. As soon as one of the draught animals gets tired, a fresh one is put at work in its place. A large force of guards, armed to the teeth, accompanies each train. The journey is accomplished in six and a half days, and the passengers are fed and lodged at the proprietor's expense. For all this, the charge is forty dollars. Those who have travelled with him speak highly of their treatment.

CHAPTER XVI.

MINING.

As regards the mineral kingdom, Mexico may be accounted the most opulent of countries. From the elaborate work which has recently been issued by the Mexican government (for a copy of which I am indebted to its courteous representative at Washington), it appears that Mexico contains all the metals known to science. The major part of these have been discovered during the present century, only seven distinct metals having been previously recognized. Now twenty-eight metals are known to exist.

Following the general direction of the Cordilleras, a metalliferous belt extends from Guanajuato to Guadalupe y Calvo, in the State of Chihuahua. Within this area are found the most important metallic deposits, commencing with those of Guaymas, in the State of Sonora, and terminating with those of Oaxaca. The sections best known for their production of gold and silver are Guanajuato, Zacatecas, Fresnillo, Real del Monte, Pachuca, Catorce, Tasco and Oaxaca.

If the importance of a mineral region is to be determined by reference to its proximity to the great centres of population, the group formed by the districts of Pachuca, Real del Monte, Atotonilco, El Chico, Capula, Santa Rosa, El Potosi and Tepeneme may be first mentioned. This group, occupying a territory which comprises fifteen and a half miles, from north to south, and of twenty and a half miles, from east to west, is only one hundred and thirty miles distant from the capital. In the next place come the district of Tasco and those of Zacuálpan, Sultepec, Angangueo, Tlalpujahua and Zimapan, which, with the mines of Oaxaca, form a circuit, opening to the eastward, around the City of Mexico, having a radius of about one hundred and thirty miles.

The districts of Guanajuato and Zacatecas, on account of their large and industrious populations, form two of the most important groups.

After these may be placed the district of Catorce, in the State of San Luis Potosi.

In the States of Sonora, Oaxaca, Michoacan, Chihuahua and Guerrero deposits abound, not only of the precious metals, but also of iron, copper, lead, zinc, etc. Hills of pure oxide of iron are found in the States of Durango and Oaxaca. Copper is found abundantly in Michoacan, Oaxaca and Chihuahua, and in the vicinity of the towns of Mazapil and Jalapa.

Mining has been so generally regarded as the chief industry of Mexico, that a work relating to that country would be considered incomplete unless some reference was made to it. It had been extensively carried on by the Aztecs, in various parts of the country, before the coming of the Spaniards; and it was the treasure of Mexico, more than anything else, that led the invaders to attempt the conquest and occupation of the country. "The Spaniards," Cortez said to the native governor at Vera Cruz, "had a disease of the heart for which gold was a specific remedy." Accordingly, after the conquest, although their commander assiduously urged them to engage in agriculture, they were not long withheld from engaging in mining enterprises.

While silver mines were the most numerous, the natives possessed gold in greater profusion. The latter was found in a natural state and is more readily wrought; whereas silver is found in combination with sulphur and with other substances, rendering an elaborate process necessary for its separation. The Spaniards were compelled to abandon many mines from which they had obtained a large yield of silver, because the supply of wood needed for smelting had been exhausted. Fortunately, a miner, Bartolomeo Medina, in the year 1557, invented the *patio* process—in other words, the art of extracting the metal by cold amalgamation—and it has since been almost universally employed. By this method of treatment, the ore is broken into small pieces with hammers and is then ground under a wheel by the help of mules. It is then reduced to a fine powder by *arrastras*, which are heavy flat stones revolving in a large vat or tub half full of water. Two weeks more are required to pulverize the ore with sufficient

Mining. 227

thoroughness. It is next mixed with chemicals, such as quicksilver, sodium chloride, *magistral*, or copper and iron sulphide. Then it is trampled upon by mules in order to mix the ingredients thoroughly. After several further manipulations, the compound is washed in water till the silver is separated. Having been reduced by heating in furnaces, it is finally cast into bars.

Prior to the discovery of the mines of California and Australia, Mexico occupied the foremost rank as regards the production of the precious metals. This was due to the largeness of the veins and to the development which has taken place within the last two centuries. The Aztecs confined themselves to working the gold mines and such others as yielded native silver. Peru, accordingly, took the palm anciently awarded to Spain herself, of being the principal silver-producing country of the world.

The *Paton Potocchi*, a silver mine of Potosi, was the greatest mine in that country, perhaps in the world; and has yielded two hundred and eighty millions of dollars.

Immediately after the conquest of Mexico,

the Spanish settlers began to work the mines of Tasco, Pachuca, Zacatecas and Guanajuato. Cortez himself, when he took up his residence at Cuernavaca, engaged in working the gold mines of Tehuantepec and the silver mines of Zacatecas. At that early period the amount of metal obtained was less than the present yield; but to compensate for this, the ore was found nearer the surface, and less expense was accordingly involved in the working. The veins are not so rich as in South America, but far excel in dimensions. The "Biscaina" at Real del Monte, near the City of Mexico, is several yards in breadth; and the main vein at Guanajuato is ten yards wide, and has been worked for a distance of more than eight miles.

The pleasantness of the climate is another great advantage. The mines of Peru are generally at a height of twelve thousand feet and more above the level of the sea, and hence in a region of almost arctic coldness; whereas the Mexican mines are seldom higher than six or seven thousand feet, where it is always temperate. The mines of Guanajuato are situated in a country producing two crops of grain each year in the valleys. Humboldt judged that about one-fifth of the silver of the world was produced from these mines. At the beginning of the last century Mexico produced annually only six or seven millions of dollars. The amount, however, was increased to thirteen millions, and, finally, at the beginning of the present century, it exceeded twenty-five millions. The yield is now less, owing to political and economic reasons; there is no limit to the opulence of the mines.

The mines of Zacatecas were early discovered. During the one hundred and eighty years ending with 1732 they produced $832,232,880. The yield at the date referred to was about $1,700,000 annually, or about one-fifth of the entire silver product of New Spain. This amount was even augmented a few years later. When the Jesuits were expelled from Mexico, the wealthy mine owners were the principal purchasers of their estates.

The mines of Guanajuato are noted for their richness. The period of their greatest prosperity was the twenty years extending from 1760 to 1780. The crown of Spain levied taxes to the amount of twenty-three million dollars each year, increasing the amount in subsequent years; and, after defraying the expenses of government, received a net revenue of one million one hundred thousand dollars.

The mine of La Valenciana, near the City of Guanajuato, produced in ten of the closing years of the last century a net profit of eight million dollars to its owners.

The famous Catorce mine in the State of San Luis Potosi was discovered in 1779. A soldier was seeking for a lost horse in the district of Charcas, when he found a large and rich " lead " of silver. The report of this discovery was made to King Charles III. by Viceroy Bucarelli. This ruler, whose reputation as a brave and upright officer has been referred to, appears to have reported many such discoveries to his royal master.

The prodigious yield of gold and silver of Mexico is readily seen when we recall the fact that the products of her mines from 1537 till

Mining. 231

1880 fall but little short of four thousand million dollars. The mines of our Western States and Territories from 1848 to 1882 yielded seventeen hundred millions of dollars of gold and five hundred and eighty-five millions of dollars of silver.

The State of Chihuahua, however, has never been fully explored. It contains one hundred and twenty mining districts, producing gold, silver, copper, lead, mercury, salt, coal, zinc, antimony, cobalt, arsenic, bismuth, nickel, and other minerals. The Mexican Central and other railroads traverse this State and will produce a revolution in mining. The scarcity of labor and the difficulties in the extraction of the ores have led to the abandoning of many rich mines, which can be again made remunerative. The completion of the Southern Pacific Railroad to El Paso in Texas increased the value of lands fourfold in Chihuahua, which indicates what is believed and expected.

The apprehension has been expressed by writers on political economy that a time will come when the production of silver will be limited, if not wholly arrested, by the depreciation of its value. Such a result was actually experienced in ancient times. When the Phœnicians brought gold from Ophir and silver from Spain, the latter was so abundant that it is recorded in Holy Scripture that the kings made it as stones in Jerusalem, and that "it was nothing accounted of in the days of Solomon."

Upon the discovery of gold in California, the demand for improved processes in mining and reducing the ore gave an impetus to invention, and the result was the construction of far more effective machinery and devices for these purposes. The introduction of American enterprise into Mexico will be doubtless characterized by the general adoption of these methods. Already the pioneer steam stamping-mill has been erected in Guanajuato, and more are certain to be set up before many years. The result can be readily foreshadowed. It is true now, though in a less degree than when Humboldt uttered it, that " the abundance of silver is such in the Cordillera chain, that one is tempted to believe that we have not begun to enjoy the inexhaustible richness that the New World contains." When the mines of Chihuahua, Sonora, Durango, Guerrero and other regions already indicated are made to reveal their profusion of the precious metal, there is risk that the wants of the world will be more than met, unless other uses both for art and taste shall be devised.

We ought not, however, to restrict our consideration of the mineral wealth of Mexico so entirely, as has been the case, to the precious metals. The country abounds with other mines of importance, which may not be overlooked. The iron mountain of Mercados, in the State of Durango, could supply all the British furnaces and foundries for more than three centuries at their present rate of consumption. This would constitute a value of one thousand million dollars—a sum representing seven times the annual coinage of gold and silver in the City of Mexico from 1690 to 1803. Chihuahua abounds with coal, copper, lead and other minerals. Coahuila contains copper and lead. Guanajuato has deposits of lead, iron, tin, cinnabar and copper. Jalisco contains lead, copper and iron. Coal and antimony are found in Michoacan. Puebla has coal and copper; San Luis Potosi has copper, lead and mercury; the Catorce district yields iron also. The same account may be given of Sinaloa. Sonora produces salt, lead, copper, iron, tin and antimony. Tamaulipas has iron, copper and lead. Zacatecas yields lead, copper, iron, sulphur, antimony, arsenic and tin. Oaxaca contains iron, copper and mercury. Chiapas has mines of lead and iron; Vera Cruz contains copper; Lower California, coal, lime, gypsum and diamonds. Petroleum is also found in many parts of the country. In short, the mineral kingdom is more abundantly represented in Mexico than in any other part of the known world; and the supply from that source alone, for both the comfort and the luxury of the human family, is very certain to be abundant for the requirements of many centuries.

CHAPTER XVII.

TO AND FROM SAN LUIS POTOSI.

THE man who drove me from Zacatecas to San Luis Potosi was not very considerate of his cattle. The road was good, and, like Jehu of old, he went along at a furious pace. All the first day the road lay through a treeless region. On account of the scarcity of water, large tracts, naturally very fertile, have been abandoned to the cactus.

The breakfast station is Ojo Caliente, a picturesque village situated at the foot of a mountain, and, for more reasons than one, resembling an oasis in the desert. The hotel fronts on a garden, immediately adjoining which is a fine park. The walls of the public-room here, as I had frequently observed elsewhere, are hung with quaint old colored engravings in heavy gilt frames, commemorative of events in Spanish annals, or of scenes from the histories of Greece and Rome. Closely examined, these engravings will often be found to be executed in the highest style of the art. Nobody seems able to give any information concerning them. It is altogether probable that they were brought from Spain while Mexico was still a province of that kingdom. They would be highly prized in New York by collectors of antique curiosities.

Having travelled eighty-four miles during the day, I reached the little town of Las Salinas, where I passed the night. As its name suggests, the manufacture of salt is the principal industry of the place. The brine for this purpose is procured from several lakes outside the town. The buildings used are enclosed by a strong wall, surrounded by a deep moat filled with water. It is spanned by a drawbridge, which is raised at night. This is a precaution against marauders and as a protection in revolutionary times. The proprietor has endeavored to beautify his property by planting trees, which have now grown to considerable size. They are the only ones to be found for many miles.

My journey the next day was for hours through an uninhabited region. Finally, however, I came to several fine *haciendas* with beautiful fields, made so by the precious endowment of nature—streams of pure running water. As I drew near the City of San Luis Potosi, the scenery became more varied, and presented a pleasing contrast with that already referred to.

After driving several miles over a straight road, I experienced a new sensation when the diligence came suddenly upon the pavements of the city. The drivers of diligences when entering or leaving a city always urge their horses or mules, as the case may be, to as rapid a pace as possible. In this instance, the concussion of the vehicle on the extremely rough pavements forced the passengers to hold tightly to the seats. The highest ambition of the diligence driver appears to be to urge his animals, eight in number, at the top of their speed, through the low, narrow entrances to the court-yards of the hotels. Failing to accomplish this feat, he must be content to take his place in the inferior ranks of his profession.

San Luis Potosi is one of the most attractive cities of Mexico. Its beautiful plaza has a fountain and a number of fine shade-trees. It is likewise adorned by a statue in bronze of Hidalgo, surmounting a pedestal of marble— the whole being about thirty feet in height. Its population is estimated to number fifty thousand, including a few Americans. What just at present gives the city especial importance is the fact that it is, by reason of its geographical position, the favorite starting-place for the United States.

Among the public buildings are the *Casa Municipal*, or City Hall, the market and the theatre. The churches possess more than ordinary architectural merit. At the date of the erection of most of them, the population was larger than it is at present. Their sculptures compare favorably with those of any other ecclesiastical edifices in Mexico. The Cathedral has a clock which was presented by one of the kings of Spain. The Sanctuary of Guadalupe is situated about a mile from the city. It is built of stone, and exhibits much architectural beauty. The Alameda, or public walk which leads to it, is a broad, paved avenue, and is embellished with shade-trees.

A military band plays at evening in the plaza, when all classes of the inhabitants come out for a promenade, thus affording an excellent opportunity to form a correct judgment of their appearance, manners and character.

The hotels are good, but an enterprising American is about to build a new one, which will be conducted like hotels in the United States. When completed it will have the distinction of being the first and only one of its kind in the Republic. It will no doubt be successful, for one soon becomes dissatisfied with the monotonous bill of fare in the hotels of Mexico.

Before the opening of the Mexican Railway (the Vera Cruz road) this city had a large overland trade, but it was then diverted into the new channels. The inhabitants are sanguine that its former importance and prosperity will be restored upon the completion of the new railroads. It is well situated on the eastern side of the great *plateau* and is easy of access from every point. Besides the two great North and South lines, a railroad is now in process of construction from Tampico on the eastern coast, a distance of three hundred and twenty-five miles. The property-owners here are heavily taxed for the payment of a subsidy for its construction. It is believed that a good harbor can be formed at Tampico by the expenditure of two million dollars. I cannot speak intelligently in regard to that matter. At present there is less than six feet of water off the bar at low tide. The Tampico river, however, is a navigable stream with good facilities for wharfage for a distance of twenty-five to thirty miles from its mouth.

The people here seem to feel very certain that when these improvements are completed their city will eclipse the capital of the Republic, not only as a centre of trade, travel and transportation, but also of population. It certainly is superior to it in regard to climate and natural advantages. The water-supply is good and the topography unsurpassed. The mines in this region were once regarded as the richest in the world, and it is thought that a judicious expenditure of capital would restore their former reputation. The ore, however, is somewhat refractory to the old Spanish methods, and the mines become overflowed with water, at only a short distance below the surface. Gold, silver, copper, lead, iron and mercury are the principal metallic productions. The present indications seem to justify many of the predictions of the inhabitants. Hence travellers and explorers are becoming too numerous for the facilities for their transportation and entertainment.

The diligence for the north leaves only three times a week. The managers do not perceive the utility of more frequent trips, although a daily coach would be crowded with passengers. Nobody appears to have the enterprise to establish a rival line. I was compelled to wait several days before I could obtain a seat, and there were several American passengers who had been delayed for more than a week from the same cause.

It takes five days to make the journey to Monterey. The rates of fare are reasonable, but the freight charges are extortionate. Each passenger is allowed to carry baggage weighing one *arroba*, which is equal to twenty-five pounds. The charge for every additional *arroba* is six dollars.

I left San Luis Potosi at four o'clock in the morning, and consequently drove for some time before the sun appeared above the horizon. Then a rapturous vision was at once displayed, and the great *plateau*, with its fringe of lofty mountains, was seen in all its glory.

One of my fellow-passengers was a German. He was a man of prepossessing appearance, and was ready to engage in conversation. He had no eye, however, for the scenery which I was admiring. By profession he was a musical composer, and his whole discourse was of pianos. He was making a journey through the country for the purpose of tuning them, and his heart was certainly in his work. "When I travels," said he, "I care nothing for scenery, or anything—only pianos. One time in Central America I see a volcano with fire come out of it, but I wouldn't look at it; I think only of pianos. When I go into a place and find no pianos there, I go me right out again, quick, always."

Having travelled a little way farther, one of the braces in the running gear of the vehicle gave way, and a considerable time was required to repair it and make a new start. Consequently, it was not till long after twelve o'clock that I arrived at the breakfast station.

Resuming the journey, I passed through a town named Montezuma. Grapes are cultivated here and a red wine is manufactured from them. Whenever the diligence stops to change mules, it is immediately surrounded by a throng of persistent, troublesome and wretched-looking beggars. Nearly all of them are crippled, diseased, old, and unable to work.

At night the diligence stopped at the town of Charcas. Here there is a very good hotel, but no wonders or curiosities are to be seen. It is the immemorial custom at hotels in Mexico never to get dinner for travellers till eight o'clock. Supplication avails nothing; bribery, for a wonder, is equally unavailing. If the proprietor is asked for dinner, he will reply, "Immediately;" but the assurance amounts to absolutely nothing. On one occasion, after receiving the promise of a speedy preparation of a meal, I walked out into the town, and was absent a full hour and a half. On my return, I found that not the slightest attention had been paid to the matter; everything was going on in the old slow style. Twenty minutes more passed before the repast was placed on the table.

I could take no solace of walking at Charcas. There was nothing curious or interesting to be seen. The diligence had arrived late; everybody was tired and hungry, eager to dine and get to bed. We appealed to the magnanimity, the humanity, the cupidity of the persons employed about the hotel. All were unavailing. They seemed to care more for keeping unshaken their antediluvian regulation as to a prescribed hour for dinner, than for any actual suffering which they beheld. After exhausting every art that could avail among an intelligent and civilized people, the passengers, worn out with impatient longing, rose in a body, marched into the dining-room, took their seats at the table, and then clamored persistently for their dinner. We doubtless horrified everybody; at any rate we obtained our dinner twenty minutes sooner. When the repast was over, we all retired promptly to the sleeping apartments. There were not beds for all; so that some of the party were obliged to seek repose on the floor.

At three o'clock in the morning everybody was up, and ready to start. The telegraph operator informed us that there would be a worse chance at the stopping-place the next night. He had learned by wire that the diligence coming southward was full. It was due one hour before ours; the hotel was a small one and every bed was certain to be taken. We held a council at once and resolved upon a policy. We promised our driver a bribe of a dollar and a half if he would get us over the distance in an hour's less time, so that we would arrive before the other coach. This would enable the four "through passengers," who were all Americans, to secure beds. To make the matter still more certain, we likewise opened negotiations with the whipper, who was quite a boy in appearance, and offered him twenty-five cents to "encourage" the mules. The result was electrifying. The vehicle was hurried along at a speed which made everybody turn and stare, as we passed them by. An earthquake could hardly have created greater astonishment. It was the dry season, the roads were hard and there was nothing to hinder our speed; but the dust was choking. We stopped for a hasty meal at Matehuala, a town of some importance, but were in no mood to take observations. We had the satisfaction of finally accomplishing our purpose; and drove into Cedral, the stopping-place for the night, half an hour before the arrival of the Northern diligence, and so were enabled to secure for ourselves the best accommodations. It was very fortunate for us to be able to do this. The next day was Monday, the day of rest for all drivers of diligences in Mexico.

Cedral is a place of little importance, and without any of the industries or other features that make a town interesting to strangers. There are mines in the vicinity, but I found it impracticable to procure a horse or conveyance of any kind for the purpose of exploring them. This region had of old been a famous resort of robbers. The neighboring town of Catorce, (which is the Spanish word for *fourteen*,) received its name from the fact that it harbored a band of notorious brigands, fourteen in number, who were long the terror of the country.

An American physician has lived here for twenty years. He is not able to leave by reason of pecuniary disabilities, family ties and other obstacles. He speaks of Cedral as by no means an attractive place of residence, for persons of refined education.

CHAPTER XVIII.

THROUGH THE SIERRA MADRE.

As usual, we set out early in the morning from Cedral. The road lay over level ground, undiversified by a single hill, and we proceeded at a satisfactory pace. There was not a house to be seen for many miles. Seven hours had gone by when we came to a *hacienda* where we could get breakfast.

At night the coach stopped at the ranch of La Ventura. The proprietor, General Trevino, of Monterey, is a man of great consideration in the State of Nuevo Leon, and is supposed to be aspiring to the Presidency of the Republic. I have little to say in favor of his subordinates at La Ventura and the methods by which they "take in" the stranger.

The next day's journey was over a continuation of the same plain as before. Toward evening I approached the mountains, between two lofty ranges of which the road now lay. These ranges form the walls of the valley of La Angostura, better known to Americans as the battle-field of Buena Vista. Here General Zachary Taylor, with an army variously estimated at from four thousand five hundred to six thousand men, disputed the ground against President Santa Anna with a force of twenty-five thousand. The battle was fought across this valley, and in the ravine which opens out of it at right angles. There is a river-bed through which a little stream of water flows; from its eastern bank several curious hillocks, resembling artificial structures, extend to the high mountain-wall. The American guns were planted on the summits of these elevations. From one of them Captain Bragg, in obedience to the order, "A little more grape, Captain Bragg," poured forth that destructive fire which for a time made his name famous.

The slaughter on both sides was terrible. It could not well be otherwise. A son of Henry Clay there laid down his life. So did Hardin, McKees, Yell of Arkansas, and many other equally brave men, whose names were less widely known to fame. Men who have since become illustrious in American history took part in that action. Many generals of the late Civil War tried their "'prentice hands" that day in the bloody gorge.

Were the Americans victorious at the battle of Buena Vista? The newspapers throughout the United States published that they were. Historical writers have borne like testimony. The bulletins of Santa Anna, however, tell a widely different story. They relate that the Mexicans, although wearied by long marching, were yet eager to meet the invaders. The progress of the battle is duly recorded, and the dismay which the resolute Mexicans produced in the ranks of their foes is eloquently portrayed.

Several weeks ago I met General Abner Doubleday of the United States Army, and I asked his judgment upon the point in question. He had served in the war with Mexico, and was present at the battle of Buena Vista. He is accurate and scrupulously truthful in his statements. The General delineated the relative positions of the two armies and the centres of interest in the conflict. He concluded with the acknowledgment that, according to the laws of military science, the position of the respective armies at the close of the action was equivalent to a victory for the Mexicans. Be this as it may, the practical result was that of victory for the Americans. General Taylor held his ground, and the whole *plateau* of Anahuac virtually fell into his hands. Had he but followed up the advantage, he, and not General Scott, would have dictated terms to the Mexican Republic in its own capital. Unfortunately, wars are directed by Cabinets, where political, rather than patriotic, influences hold sway. General Taylor was remanded into idleness, and a new campaign more costly and more murderous was instituted to extend from Vera Cruz to the capital of Mexico. This scheme, however, resulted adversely to those by whom it was concocted.

The day's drive brought me to Saltillo, the capital of the State of Coahuila. At this point the great *plateau* suddenly terminates with a precipitous cliff. The city lies beneath, and nobody approaching it from the south would suspect its existence till, on descending the slope by the winding road, he had entered its streets. It is an old town, begun in 1586, and was created a city in 1827. At first it was called Leona Vicario, in honor of a heroine of the Mexican War of Independence. The designation, however, was not popular; and now the name Saltillo, an old Chichemec word, has usurped its place. It signifies "a highland with abundant water"; and, indeed, it merits the appellation. The city has about twenty thousand inhabitants.

When under the Spanish dominion, the State of Coahuila was known as the province of Nueva Estremadura, and included part of Texas, as far as the Medina river. After independence had been established, Coahuila was included in the same State with Texas; but, after the final alienation of that territory by the treaty of 1848, it was made into a commonwealth by itself. Later it was joined to Nuevo Leon, but in 1868 again became a separate government.

At the present time there are two stage-coach

lines running northward from Saltillo. One of these, which is owned by an American, has daily coaches.

From Saltillo to Monterey the scenery is magnificent. The road extends through a valley several miles wide that has the appearance of being much narrower, and is walled in on both sides by the steep slopes of grand old mountains, wild and picturesque, belonging to the Sierra Madre. The trees upon these mountains are meagre and of insignificant dimensions, and are far from concealing the crags, which often exhibit the most fantastic shapes.

This range of mountains is very rich in minerals. The valley is abundantly watered by the numerous streams from the summits, and is generally fertile. The road gradually but steadily descends, as it extends northward. It is traversed continually by heavy wagons that are employed for the carrying trade between Saltillo and Monterey. They are drawn by mules, ten or fourteen to a wagon. The track of the road is thus cut up fearfully, and a prodigious quantity of dust is constantly flying.

The inn, where the diligence stopped for refreshment, is situated on a hill which overlooks a farm, and the fields of waving grain afford a vivid delight to one who has journeyed for days where little vegetation can be seen except the cactus. The white buildings of Monterey, twenty-five miles distant, could be distinctly seen. In the clear atmosphere they seemed to be much closer.

As I approached the end of the day's journey I came to the battle-field of Monterey. The place is now marked by a mound of earth surmounted by a plain wooden cross. Perhaps the antiquarian of some future race, now without a historical recognition, may stand here like Macaulay's typical New-Zealander and classify this eminence as a monument of the Olmecs, or some other people of unknown remoteness, and equally low in the scale of civilization.

Just behind the battle-ground, the Sierra Madre is broken by a wild and picturesque *cañon*, the rocky walls of which are broken and variegated in a most wonderful manner. They far surpass the Palisades of the Hudson for their striking appearance. It is easy, as one contemplates their marvellous variety of figures, to trace out cathedrals, needles, obelisks, sentinels, and other analogous shapes and structures.

The road lay through the valley of St. Peter. It was here that our soldiers made their way along, climbed the hill, literally forcing a passage through the terrible thorn-bushes of Osage-orange, and stormed the Bishop's palace at the summit. In this charge Lieutenant U. S. Grant distinguished himself, and received his first award of promotion. Another officer, however, who had displayed no such courage or meritorious conduct, had also received a like distinction. Grant at once declared : " If he deserves promotion, I do not ; " and proudly declined the honor.

As the diligence was passing the Bishop's palace, now a ruin, a train of cars came rapidly along on the new railroad, carrying a party of Mexican excursionists who had been riding to the end of the completed track, which now extends several miles toward Saltillo. It was a fitting prelude and augury of the new times that are coming to the Mexican people.

CHAPTER XIX.

THE RAILROADS.

THE railroad is at once the expression and the instrument of modern civilization. Perhaps in no other portion of the Western Hemisphere is it destined to play so important a part as in Mexico. Owing to the almost total absence of navigable streams throughout our sister Republic, the railroad would seem to furnish the very instrumentality which is indispensable to her future development. Fortunately for her, the great *plateau* presents an incomparable route for this mode of trade and travel. According to Humboldt, four-wheeled carriages proceed from the capital, in the centre of the *plateau*, to Santa Fé, a distance of fourteen hundred miles, without any important deviation from an apparent level.

In the humblest and most secluded hamlets, as well as in the centres of population, intelligence and wealth, the conviction has sunk deeply into the minds and hearts of the people that when the railroads, which are now in progress, shall be completed, a Golden Age will dawn upon the country. The facilities which will thus be afforded for trade, travel and transportation will, it is confidently predicted, stimulate activity and industry in every direction, so that the almost boundless natural resources of the country will be developed, and its people, in all conditions of life, will become more prosperous than ever before. These expectations might be regarded as visionary but for the lesson taught by the history of railroads in the United States.

Fifty years ago, a few feeble enterprises were inaugurated in this country with equivocal, not to say forbidding, prospects of success. Now the whole future of the nation seems to be dependent upon the gigantic companies which hold not only the internal communications, but the commerce of the country, in their hands. They control the destiny of States and Territories, as well as those of individuals and localities. What these mighty corporations and combinations have in store for us in the future, time alone can determine.

Happily, Mexico has it in her power to profit by our experience, and so to avoid the mistakes of American railroad legislation. The patriotic and able statesmen who at present have the direction of her public affairs will doubtless see to it that this result is kept steadily in view.

With the railroads, constructed and controlled by American enterprise and capital, will come two all-important benefits: first, improved processes in agriculture, mining, manufactures, and every other branch of the industrial arts; second, cheap transportation, which, by leaving to the tiller of the soil and to the toiler in the mines an increased share of the fruits of his industry, cannot fail to elevate his social, intellectual, moral and political condition.

First in the field, the Mexican Railway Company, some years ago, completed the road from Vera Cruz to Mexico, with a branch to the City of Puebla—in all, a length of two hundred and ninety-two miles. Having an ascent of over eight thousand feet to overcome, and having to contend with defective means of transporting material, the cost of construction was excessive, and reached the enormous sum of thirty million dollars; which amount, however, includes a subsidy from the Mexican Government of twelve million dollars. This aggregate, there is high authority for asserting, is fully three times as great as that for which the road could now be built. Ten millions would now suffice for this purpose. The receipts of the company have steadily increased from year to year, so that they now reach nearly five million dollars annually, which enables them to pay a dividend on the common stock of six and one-half per cent. per annum.

Its management cannot be termed liberal or far-seeing. Gross inattention to duty characterizes its subordinates. They pay no regard to punctuality or to the convenience of the travelling public. The prices charged for the transportation and storage of merchandise are exorbitant, not to say prohibitory. So far as this railway is concerned, there can be no remunerative commerce till a complete revolution in its administration shall be effected. A virtual monopoly, its management is arbitrary and oppressive. A brief statement of my experience of its exactions may not be amiss.

On the twenty-second day of March last I caused to be delivered, at the station in the City of Mexico, a wooden box which contained several specimens of ancient pottery, packed for security in shavings. It was addressed to my father, at New York, and was consigned to the distinguished commercial firm of Messrs. R. C. Ritter & Co., in the City of Vera Cruz, the company executing a receipt for it accordingly. This receipt I retained in my possession as a measure of security. The dimensions and weight of the package were as follows:

Length ....25 inches.
Width ....$11\frac{1}{2}$ "
Height................12 "
Weight...16 kilograms, or $35\frac{1}{4}$ lbs.

I gave the consignees immediate notice, by letter, of the shipment; but, as I was constantly travelling through the country, they were unable to communicate with me.

On my return to this city, I learned that the company refused to surrender the box, unless this receipt was shown to them. Accordingly they held it for six weeks, and then charged the sum of four dollars and sixty-three cents for storage. But this was not all. They exacted, in addition, the sum of one dollar, under the designation of *guaranty for delivery without receipt.* The package had been roughly handled, and the largest and most valuable of the contents was broken. The package being of the second class, freight was charged at the rate of one dollar and fifty cents per cwt. The distance over which it was transported was two hundred and sixty-four miles. The exorbitancy of this charge will be rendered apparent by the following statement. The investigation of what is known as the Hepburn Committee of the Legislature of the State of New York showed that merchandise can be profitably transported by rail from the City of New York to Chicago, a distance of nine hundred and eighty miles, for the sum of fifteen cents per cwt. Of course, the charge of the Mexican Railway Company is about forty times as great.

When the box was finally placed on board the "British Empire" steamer, of the Alexandre Line, at Vera Cruz, the charges on it, including the sum of three dollars for the consular certificate, amounted to the sum of ten dollars and thirteen cents. If to this amount be added a very moderate estimate for correspondence, postage, and bother generally, the aggregate would reach at least ten times the value of the property. I leave it for others to determine whether a railway conducted like this one is likely to prosper, or, indeed, ought to prosper.

The Mexican Central Railroad Company has agreed to construct a road of the standard gauge from the City of Mexico to Leon, and from Leon to the northern frontier, making connection with Aguas Calientes, Zacatecas, and Chihuahua. The company further agrees to construct the road from a point intermediate between the cities of Mexico and Leon, to some point on the Pacific coast, connecting on the way with the City of Guadalajara. The charter, or "concession," is for the period of ninety-nine years, after which the road will become the property of the Mexican Government. The latter agrees to pay for all other property of the company on a valuation as provided for, and also to give the company the preference in case of a determination at the expiration of the time specified to sell or lease the road. The charter originally obligated the completion of the track from the City of Mexico to Leon in 1882, to the Pacific within five years, and to Paso del Norte by 1891. A bond of $250,000 was required to be deposited in the City of Mexico for the due fulfilment of these conditions. It is expected, however, that the main line will be completed by July, 1884.

I rode over the southern section of this road, as far as completed, when on my way to the North. It has been built from the City of Mexico as far north as Lagos, and from the City of Chihuahua to the frontier. The Government has recently modified the conditions of the charter, extending the time for the completion of the lines, as well as the exemptions and privileges. The subsidy is also to be increased from September, 1884, provided the main line to Paso del Norte is then completed. The company is also authorized to increase the tariff on the interoceanic line from Tampico to San Blas; and the discount on transportation for the Government is reduced from sixty to forty per cent. The forfeiture clause is revoked and a fine is substituted in lieu thereof.

The region traversed by this road is one of the most important in the country. Immediately after leaving the City of Mexico, the line enters the fertile valley of Tula; beyond which is another opulent district, comprising the valleys of Huichapam, San Juan del Rio, and others. Beyond Queretaro are the plains of Bajio, where irrigation at seed-time assures enormous crops of grain. Artesian wells can easily be multiplied and cultivation extended, till the entire plains shall become a garden.

Political reasons have probably dictated the

selection of San Blas, in the State of Jalisco, as the western terminus. It is regarded as very desirable to effect the early colonizing of that region, and the completion of the road is expected to secure this end. The country is agricultural, with a tropical climate; and the valleys of Ameca, Ahualulco, Etzatlan, Tequila and Magdalena are rich beyond comparison in cereals, sugar, and other products. The plantations will be more thoroughly cultivated, and their productiveness will be correspondingly increased as soon as the road goes into operation.

This road passes along the axis of a zone having an average width of fifteen leagues, which lies between the rivers Tololatlan and Ameca, with a fertile soil and semi-tropical climate admirably adapted to the cultivation of cotton, coffee, rice and sugar. These rivers also furnish abundant water-power, which can be employed with advantage in the mechanical arts.

Agricultural products do not, however, constitute the only tributaries of this route. At Tula the road will receive the ores and minerals coming from Zimapan, El Cardonal, Jacala, and Encarnacion. At San Juan del Rio it will likewise receive a large part of the mineral product of the Sierra Gorda. In approaching Guanajuato it enters a metalliferous region, perhaps the most important in the country, which is now actively worked. Guanajuato itself also is a city of much wealth, and having an extensive trade with the interior. At Salamanca there are abundant deposits of kaolin and white clay, which will either constitute an article of export, or else manufactories of porcelain will be established for supplying the wants of the country. Leon will furnish stone for building and ornamental purposes in inexhaustible quantities.

Extending beyond Leon to the north, the road traverses a belt productive of the cereals. The plains of Tecuan have a rich soil, capable, with the aid of irrigation, of abundant fertility. This want artesian wells can be made to supply. The valley of Aguas Calientes, which extends beyond the city of that name, is almost exactly parallel with the valley of Rio de San Pedro. It can not only produce cereals in abundance, but it contains extensive forests of timber valuable for building and for ornamental purposes. The route of the road proceeds from Aguas Calientes to Zacatecas, and thence onward toward Durango. There is no stipulation in the charter to include Durango in the route, but it is convenient to do so, and the region is capable of being made highly productive. Cotton, sugar-cane and the cereals can be profitably cultivated on a large scale. The same may be said of the other regions and plains which the road will traverse on the way to El Paso. At that point it connects with the Southern Pacific Railroad of the United States. The charter provides that a branch of the Central Railroad shall be extended from San Luis Potosi to Tampico. It will also connect the former place with Queretaro or Zacatecas. This will place the States of the interior in direct railway communication with the seaboard. Their mineral and agricultural products will thus find an outlet, and there will be a corresponding influx of goods of foreign manufacture. The facility of transit will enlarge the area of production and consumption, the direct tendency of which will be to attract thither a large accession of immigrants.

The Mexican Central will, when completed, connect with the Atchison, Topeka and Santa Fé system. It is well managed, and is already well Americanized, the officials of the road and the persons employed being mostly Americans. The English language is spoken almost exclusively. The signs and notices are generally printed in both the English and the Spanish languages. What is true of the Mexican Central will be found equally so of the other projected railroads which are intimately connected with the railroad systems of the United States. The English language is likely to predominate, as well as the American methods of management.

CHAPTER XX.

THE RAILROADS—CONTINUED.

THE Mexican National Railway, now in process of construction, is a narrow-gauge road. When the necessary communication shall be completed through Texas, it will connect with the Texas and St. Louis narrow-gauge system, so as practically to form part of it. The contract with the Mexican National Construction Company provides for the constructing and operating of a narrow-gauge railroad from the City of Mexico to the Pacific Ocean at the port of Manzanillo or Navidad, passing through the cities of Toluca, Maravatio, Acambaro, Morelia, Zamora, and La Piedad. Furthermore, it provides for a branch or line from the City of Mexico northward, to leave the Pacific line at a point between Maravatio and Morelia, and pass through the cities of San Luis Potosi, Saltillo and Monterey to any point which may be selected on the Rio Grande, between Laredo and Eagle Pass. The term of the charter is ninety-nine years, the Government obligating itself to rent or sell its own rights to the Company, as agreed upon under the "concession" of September 13th, 1880.

The company agrees to complete the line to the Pacific in five years, and that to the frontier in eight years, from the date of the charter. The whole length of the proposed line is one thousand seven hundred and sixty-seven miles. A subvention of $7,000 per kilometre, or $11,266 per mile, has been granted by the Mexican Government for the line extending from the capital to the Pacific; and of $6,500 per kilometre, or $10,462 per mile, for the southern branch. The distance from the junction to Laredo is eleven hundred and twenty-five kilometres — making the total amount of the subvention for the latter $7,312,500. Trains are now running from Laredo to Monterey, and the road will be opened this summer as far as Saltillo. When I visited the volcano of Jorullo, I rode over the southern line as far as Maravatio, in the State of Michoacan. The line has since been opened to Acambaro, and the roadway has been graded as far as Patzcuaro, a distance of forty-two miles from Morelia and two hundred and twenty-three miles from the capital. The grades near the City of Mexico are very steep, the maximum elevation which is reached being nine thousand nine hundred and seventy-four feet.

The territory which the route of the National Railway traverses is in no respect inferior to that which is tributary to the Mexican Central. The southern branch, until it approaches Lake Chapala, penetrates the section of country which is drained by the Rio de Lerma. It proceeds around that lake through a highly fertile region to the salt plains of Zacoalco and Sayula, and then enters the district lying between the rivers Armeria and Coahuayana. There are several lakes of considerable size in this vicinity. The great agricultural and mineral wealth of these regions is well understood. All varieties of climate from tropical to frigid, and the productions of every zone, are found there. There are large plantations of sugar and coffee, and gold, silver, iron, copper and quicksilver are abundant. Descending the Pacific slope, the Mexican National Railway passes through the rich tropical region lying south of the State of Jalisco, including the States of Michoacan and Colima. Sugar and coffee are abundantly produced here, and the quality of the latter, like that of Cordova, is highly prized wherever it is known.

Valuable forests likewise abound in this region, and extensive tracts suited to grazing purposes are found in the States of Mexico, Michoacan, Colima and Jalisco. The last named State has, in addition, many rich mines. Indeed, the section of country which this line and the Central will render accessible is not surpassed, as regards mineral wealth, in the Republic.

In consideration of the subsidies which it receives, this company is required to restrict its charges for the transportation of passengers, produce, and merchandise to the rates prescribed by law. Its authorized charge for merchandise is as follows: First class, four cents a ton per kilometre; second class, three cents; third class, two cents. For passengers: First class, two and a half cents per kilometre, or four cents a mile; second class, two cents per kilometre, or about three and one-fifth cents a mile; third class, one cent per kilometre, or about one and a half cents a mile. Cereals must be carried at the rate of three and a quarter cents a ton per mile. Forty per cent. must be deducted from the regular rates for the transportation of articles for the Government. For the military forces, individuals employed by the Federal authorities, and immigrants coming under Federal authorization, the same deduction is required to be made. In case of forfeiture of the charter, the road becomes the property of the Government at its appraised value, after deducting subsidies; and the franchise must again be sold.

The Morelos Railway is owned by residents of Mexico. In the face of many discouragements, including serious engineering difficulties, it was begun by Señor Sanchez, the President of the Tehuantepec Railroad, in 1879. The route extends over the marshes which border the lakes in the valley of Mexico, and thence along the base of the mountains to a populous region of great natural wealth, but one which is rarely visited by foreigners. It extends to the City of Cuautla de Morelos. Despite the gloomy predictions that money could not be had and that the road would not pay expenses, it is in operation and doing a good business, chiefly in freights. Señor Sanchez insists that he will be able before many years to extend the Morelos Railway to Acapulco. He richly deserves success.

The charter of the Tehuantepec Railroad was originally granted to Edward Larned, of the City of New York, in 1879. It has since been forfeited, and Señor Sanchez is endeavoring, under the auspices of the Mexican Government, to procure money in this country in order to prosecute the work of construction. He is a man of indomitable will and energy, as has been already shown, and little doubt exists that before many years the Isthmus Road will be finished.

The Mexican Southern Railway Company, of which General Grant is the President, will traverse the coffee and sugar districts of Southern Mexico. Its initial point is the port of Anton Lizardo, which lies sixteen miles to the south of Vera Cruz. The harbor is pronounced the best on the Gulf of Mexico, the only obstacle with which it has to contend being the coral reefs off the coast. A branch of the road will connect the two places. The main line extends from Anton Lizardo, in a south-westerly direction, by way of Tuxtepec and Amana, to Arenal. This is the highest elevation anywhere on the route, being fifty-five hundred feet above the level of the sea. Thence it proceeds, in a southern direction, by way of Cuicatlan and Sedas, to Oaxaca. From Oaxaca it will run in a south-westerly direction, by way of Ejutla and Miahuatlan, to the town of Tehuantepec. It then takes an easterly course to Tonala, where it forks, one division extending to Tapachula, in the State of Chiapas, and then into Guatemala; the other to San Christobal and in the direction of Chiquimaceto. A branch line will extend from Arenal in a north-western direction to Puebla, there connecting with the International and Interoceanic Railway.

No part of the Southern Railway has yet been built. Work is, however, in progress for the purpose of improving the harbor of Anton Lizardo. There will be little difficulty in the way of grading. The greatest ascent is seventy-two feet per mile. There has been no grading done as yet; indeed the construction of this road will depend largely upon the completion of the International and Interoceanic.

General Diaz, Ex-President of the Republic, and now Governor of Oaxaca, takes a warm interest in this enterprise. His State will be traversed by the new road, and is certain to be benefited by its construction.

The International and Interoceanic Railway Company at its inception was a part of the south-west system of the United States which comprised about seven thousand miles of road-bed, belonging to the Missouri Pacific, the Texas Pacific, the Missouri, Kansas and Texas, the Iron Mountain, the International and Great

Northern, and the New Orleans and Pacific. The route of the road in Mexico extends from Laredo to the City of Mexico, by way of Guerrero, Mier Santander, Jimenes, Victoria, and Jalancingo, with the option of building branches to Vera Cruz, Tampico, and Matamoros. That part of the line which extends through the State of Tamaulipas is easy of construction; but, immediately upon reaching Victoria, there are mountain ranges to encounter which will render the work more difficult and expensive.

This route has been chosen with characteristic shrewdness. It traverses a region which is considered among the most desirable in Mexico, in respect both to agricultural products and mineral wealth; and ample returns for the investment are assured. It will connect, as already stated, with the authorized route of the Mexican Southern at Puebla. The two schemes have recently been consolidated under conditions that are regarded as very advantageous to both. The *Official Journal* of the City of Mexico for May 28, 1883, has published the contract between the Mexican Government, Jay Gould and General Grant, governing their consolidation. It guarantees all the benefits heretofore granted, and modifies the clause relating to forfeiture, making it more favorable to the united companies.

The Mexican Railway Company (the Vera Cruz road), which has thus far enjoyed a monopoly of railroad transportation in the country, has complained of this measure, as an act of bad faith on the part of the Mexican Government, but it is hardly probable that any serious obstacle will be interposed in the way of the consolidated companies.

General Grant has expressed the opinion that the principal route from the United States will be by the Atchison, Topeka, and Santa Fé Railroad to El Paso, and thence by the Mexican Central Railroad to the City of Mexico. He is thoroughly familiar with Mexico. During the war between that country and the United States he was an officer under General Taylor, and was in the battles of Brownsville, Palo Alto, Resaca de la Palma, and Monterey. The regiment to which he belonged was then transferred to the command of General Scott. It was sent down the Rio Grande to its mouth, and from thence was forwarded by steamer and man-of-war to Vera Cruz. They were landed on the Island of Sacrifices. General Scott first reduced the Castle of San Juan de Ulloa, and then marched his forces, by way of Jalapa, Perote, and Puebla, to the City of Mexico. They first encountered General Santa Anna at Cerro Gordo between Jalapa and Vera Cruz. General Grant took part in all the engagements from that point to the capital.

Among the railways at present in progress which will be tributary to the Mexican system is the Central Transit Railway of Texas. The proposed line rests upon a charter from the State of Texas. Its length is about five hundred miles, the initial point being at Shreveport, Louisiana, where it connects with the Erlanger system, and its terminus at the Rio Grande, near Eagle Pass, where it will connect with some of the projected Mexican roads.

The recently completed surveys of the route have resulted in obtaining a line singularly direct and remarkably free from any heavy grades. Its entire route is in a temperate climate, of remarkable fertility from end to end, and embracing every variety of production, thus insuring throughout an abundant local traffic.

Connecting on the Rio Grande with the lines already projected to the Pacific, near the mouth of the Gulf of California, it is an important link in the shortest route between the two oceans, and intersects the entire railroad system east of the Mississippi river.

The Pacific ocean steamers, or other vessels sailing from San Francisco for China, usually follow the ocean currents and sail south on their outward voyage about eighteen hundred miles to the latitude of Mazatlan and the mouth of the Gulf of California before taking a westward course, via the Sandwich Islands, to Hong-Kong. Mazatlan is the nearest point on the American continent to Australia.

European travel, by way of the United States, to Mazatlan, the Sandwich Islands, Hong-Kong and Australia, will have the advantage of some three thousand miles by the Central Transit route over the northern lines, without the interruption of an hour in the year from climatic impediments. This line will consequently command the through business and commerce of Europe and Asia, in addition to a local business of constantly increasing importance and value.

Having passed over nearly every railroad now in operation, as well as over portions of those which are in process of construction in all parts of Mexico, I have no hesitation in saying that, with the single exception of the Mexican Railway, I have found them well managed and apparently doing a prosperous business. In many ways I have had it in my power to ascertain the views of the people in general regarding them.

I have repeatedly come in contact with travellers who were making wide detours, involving the expenditure of both time and money, in order that they might enjoy what they regarded as the luxury of railroad travelling, and at the same time escape the annoyances of diligence and horseback locomotion. In short, if the Mexicans shall have the good fortune to reap even a small proportion of the benefits which they fondly anticipate from the completion of the several works now under way, what has been styled "The Railway Invasion" will prove to be the greatest boon which has ever fallen to the lot of our sister Republic.

CHAPTER XXI.

MONTEREY.

THE drive into Monterey was through green fields and gardens. All the surroundings were in pleasing contrast with the barren plains which I had passed over during the previous day's journey. Being now in a region of comparatively small elevation above the sea-level, the difference of climate was at once perceptible.

The diligence brought me to the gate of the Hotel Iturbide. Here it was stopped; the usual narrow entrance, curiously reminding me of the *needle's eye* of the Scripture, was not open for coaches. A garden now occupies the place of the former court-yard; so that while the passengers were permitted to enter by the covered way, the driver was compelled, after they had left the vehicle, to go round on the outside of the building, to the stable in the rear.

The two principal hotels of Monterey are

kept by American proprietors, and are patronized by all travellers from the United States. The bill of fare at the Hotel Iturbide is a combination of both the American and Mexican styles of cookery. Crowds of people are constantly coming and going; and day after day there is an incessant strife to secure rooms. Cots are every night set up in the corridors, and activity is apparent on every hand. Everybody is busy, and the new-comer receives little attention. He is left generally to his own choice whether to wait an hour for a porter, or to carry his baggage to his room for himself. Again I was reminded that "coming events cast their shadows before."

Having now completed the overland journey by diligence, I decided to rest here a few days before going farther. My chief amusement was to observe the numerous parties of American tourists who came down by the railroad from points in Texas and the South-west. They were the only persons of their class that I had met in the Mexican Republic. When they arrived and had become a little settled, the first thing they did was to go out and make purchases. They generally returned with a *zarape*, or Mexican blanket, and a fancy basket. The baskets are made by the prisoners confined in the jail. This building was formerly the Convent of San Francisco. There are many American residents in Monterey, and, if any one is unable to speak Spanish and needs an interpreter, he can easily find somebody who will cheerfully help him.

Monterey and its environs are full of interest. The scenery is magnificent. The city lies in a valley between the *Cerro de la Silla*, or Saddle-Mountain, on one side, and *La Mitra*, or the Mitre, on the other. These mountains rise to the height of about four thousand feet above the sea-level, while the valley has an elevation of but sixteen hundred and twenty-six feet. A small stream of water runs through the city and is crossed by a substantial bridge which played an important part in the war with the United States. It was the scene of a sanguinary engagement, and was successfully held by the Mexicans against the assaults of the American forces.

The exact date of the founding of the city is not known. It first bore the name of Santa Lucia, afterwards that of Leon. When the city was begun, the untamed Indian tribes had been but recently expelled from the region. The newly acquired territory took the name of the New Kingdom of Leon. This city was the capital. In the year 1596 it was duly constituted as the metropolis of Our Lady of Monterey. It now has a cathedral, several fine churches, a convent and a public library.

The American Board of Foreign Missions has maintained a station at Monterey for many years, and its representatives have had a fair share of success. The Baptists also have their missionaries in the field, and enforce their religious ideas with great zeal. It is probable that the City of Monterey will become the centre and focus of the Protestant worship in future years.

It was now time to bid farewell to Mexico. No more diligence riding! The railroad has entered the Republic from the north, and a train of cars takes passengers to the Rio Grande in twelve hours. For many miles out from Monterey, the scenery is of the most attractive character, with the grand Sierra Madre constantly in view. Later, all this is changed. The train passes through an entirely different region. All that can now be seen, is a vast plain covered with the Osage-orange and the cactus. In the springtime, however, the monotony is somewhat relieved; for then the cactus is in blossom. The flowers are of varied hues, yellow, orange, red and purple, and the tints are often of great splendor.

At length, the train approached the town of Nuevo Laredo. Its high frame buildings, so totally unlike the stuccoed houses of other Mexican cities, and its general appearance proclaimed the influence of another people. At sunset I crossed the Rio Grande and entered Laredo, the frontier city. I was once more in the United States.

CHAPTER XXII.

THE FUTURE OF MEXICO.

No discerning man can fail to perceive that the destiny of our own country is to be, hereafter, closely interwoven with that of Mexico. Besides, the cause of free government and its adaptation to all conditions of men will henceforth be on trial before the world as perhaps it never has been before.

The Mexican Minister at Washington estimates the population of Mexico at ten million souls. He classifies them as follows:

Number of inhabitants of pure Spanish lineage 1,000,000
Number of inhabitants of mixed blood, including Mestizos, Zambos, Quadroons and Octoroons 4,000,000
Number of aborigines, commonly designated as Indians................ 5,000,000

The last-named class differs in many respects from the Indians who are found within the limits of the United States. An officer of the United States Army, who has seen much service among the savage tribes of the West, gives it as his opinion that an American Indian, living, as he does, chiefly by the chase, requires a territorial area of forty square miles for his support. Every effort to eradicate his love for a nomadic life, or in any way to civilize him, has thus far proved vain and impotent.

The aborigines of Mexico, on the other hand, are, without exception, stationary, and are addicted to manual labor of some kind. It will, of course, be understood that the Comanches and Apaches, whose reservations lie exclusively within the United States, but who are in the habit of crossing the border when pursued by the military, are not included in this designation. An average of two or three acres, in other words, the one ten-thousandth part of the above-named quantity of land, suffices to support each Mexican man, woman and child. Descended, as they are, directly from the Aztecs, who, under the

Montezumas, attained an advanced civilization, their whole mode of life antagonizes that of the American savage. It is stated that they are divided into various tribes, and I have heard the number of these placed as high as twenty.

Señor Romero describes them as follows: " I have not seen any people more docile and more deserving of a better fate than the Indians of Mexico. They are ignorant and poor for reasons that I have already set forth, but there are elements in them to make them a great people. Whenever any one of the race has had advantages of education, he has risen to the highest standard. Many of Mexico's most distinguished men, either as statesmen, patriots, soldiers, etc., have been pure-blooded Indians, as Juarez and Morelos. I have the highest sympathy for them, and I would spare no effort to do them justice and to advance their condition in every way I possibly could. I believe one of the most effective means to obtain this result is to increase their wages; and this has already been one of the first effects of railroad building in Mexico. When they are well off they will be a different people from what they are now."

The all-important problem which awaits solution, in the future of Mexico, is: *By what means can the welfare of these millions be most effectually promoted?* My reference here is to the *nine millions*, and not to the *one million*. Upon the success or failure of the present rulers of Mexico to solve this momentous problem will depend both the estimation in which they are held by their contemporaries at home and abroad, and their just claim to an honorable place on the page of history.

When California was acquired by the United States, the number of Mexicans within its borders probably did not exceed, in all, twenty thousand. The number of adult males, accordingly, hardly reached five thousand. Very soon after the opening of the gold-fields, at least ten times that number of adventurers from Europe, and from all parts of the Western Hemisphere, precipitated themselves upon the country.

The character and purpose of the vast majority of these men are too well known to require comment. The result was that everything Mexican was at once eliminated from the soil of California. Still, it may be doubted whether the charges which from time to time have been made, of interference with the then established forms of religious worship, can be substantiated. The truth is that the missions of the Roman Catholic Church had, for the most part, fallen into decay, and the number of communicants had been correspondingly diminished, before the descent of the gold-hunters upon the country.

Whatever else may happen, effectual measures should be adopted to guard against the possibility of enacting a similar drama on the soil of Mexico. Surely no man of generous and philanthropic views can, for a moment, countenance any scheme which will ignore the rights of the millions of that country. Least of all will those of our own countrymen, who, twenty years ago, fought in the fore-front of freedom's battle, consent to so foul a wrong.

Since the acquisition of California, the greatest triumph for personal liberty that history has recorded—the emancipation of four millions of slaves—has been achieved in this country. Let us hope that the great principles of human rights which have been written in blood on that monument of freedom, the Constitution of the United States, will be enforced, so far as the people of our sister republic are concerned. On many a bloody field the Mexicans have proved their innate and inextinguishable love for liberty. Let it be understood from the outset that the new departure is for their advantage, and not, in any sense, for their oppression.

In a conversation with General Grant, on the subject of my tour through Mexico, he remarked that the present is an interesting period for visiting that country, as many and great changes are about to occur there. The premonitions on every hand indicate the correctness of this remark. It is within my personal knowledge that many of our people are about to engage in mining, manufactures, agriculture and in other industrial pursuits, at various points throughout the republic.

Hotels, to be conducted on the American

plan, will be erected in several of the large centres of population and business. Horses, horned cattle and sheep are to be raised on an extensive scale. The culture of the vine and the manufacture of wine will be introduced at an early day on the Pacific slope. Agricultural implements will be made at various points, and furnished to the tiller of the soil at prices which will at once create for them an extensive market. Vehicles of all descriptions, from a simple two-wheeled cart to a fashionable carriage, will be made, not only in the capital, but in several other places; thus providing the means to establish, as proposed by President Gonzalez, innumerable local channels for the transportation of the products of the soil and mines on the one hand, and of manufactured goods on the other. These avenues will be tributary to the great lines of railroad. Sugar refineries will be established, in the neighborhood of the sugar-cane plantations, on both the east and west of the country. Petroleum refineries will be opened in the State of Vera Cruz and at points on the Pacific coast. The manufacture of the rich ornamental woods, the mahogany, the ebony, and the rosewood, which in some places are now used for fuel, will become before long an important branch of industry.

Of course, the mining of iron, copper and quicksilver, as well as that of the precious metals, will be prosecuted with the aid of the most improved machinery, on a more extensive scale than ever before. Smelting-furnaces and rolling-mills will soon follow.

Tobacco, Indian corn, coffee, sugar, cotton, wheat, indigo, vanilla, sarsaparilla, jute, hemp, etc., will be produced more extensively than they have been heretofore, because all will be certain to find a ready and profitable market, both at home and abroad.

Enough has been said to show that, for the first time since the Spanish Conquest, the Mexicans are to be favored with a diversified industry. How shall this change be turned to their highest advantage? How shall it be made to inure to their elevation, moral, intellectual, political and social?

The elementary writers on the science of government define a republic to be that form of government in which the administration of public affairs is open to all the citizens. We are accustomed to call Mexico a republic. Is it so in fact? I am of the opinion that it is a republic only in name. After a sojourn of considerable duration in the country, during which I visited the more populous districts, the government appears to me to be practically an oligarchy. I make this statement with the less reserve, because I miss in the civil polity of Mexico, that clear and distinct recognition of the essential dignity of human nature and of the superiority of the rights of manhood to the rights of property, which constitute the vital essence of our own political system. I miss, besides, the guaranty of religious freedom which is contained in the Constitution of the United States, and which is even more fully embodied in the Constitution of the State of New York in these memorable words: "The free exercise and enjoyment of religious profession and worship, without discrimination or preference, shall forever be allowed in this State to all mankind."

The truth is that the inequalities of condition are nearly as great in Mexico to-day as they were during the Spanish domination, or as they are at this moment in any country of continental Europe. The land belongs almost wholly to the white race. When it is cultivated in small parcels by the Indians, the usual custom is to give one-half of the product to the landlord as rent.

Unquestionably, the most effectual of all the plans which have been suggested for ameliorating the condition of the peons is to make them the owners of the soil. By this means the present system of tillage will undergo a radical change. Instead of living, as they do at present, in cities or hamlets, the tillers of the soil will occupy the land which they own. A large increase in the crops will inevitably ensue. But what is perhaps of still greater importance, is the change which will be wrought in the status of the farmer. Better food, better clothing and a better house will supersede his present surroundings. With these will come a greater degree of interest in the administration of public affairs, growing out of his increased stake in the preservation of social order. The standing army and the rural police may then be reduced, because self-government will take the place of the repressive measures which are now in force. Then, and not till then, will Mexico take her place as a model republic, beside the United States of America.

www.ingramcontent.com/pod-product-compliance
Lightning Source LLC
Chambersburg PA
CBHW022021240426

43667CB00042B/1046